Cat Kist

In memory of Rita Hardy Ramsden
Whose friendship meant so much to the fortunate

And for Wimpey

Cat Kist

The Redbeck Anthology
of Contemporary Cats

Edited by
Jane Ramsden

Cat Kist is published by Redbeck Press,
24 Aireville Road, Frizinghall, Bradford
BD9 4HH.

Design and print by Rollia Printers Ltd,
Red Oak House, Duncombe Street,
Bradford BD8 9AJ.

Typeset by Kath Leaver,
67 Moorhead Crescent, Moorhead,
Shipley, West Yorkshire BD18 4LQ.
Tel: 07976 950 447

Cat Kist
ISBN 1-904338-27-5

A CIP catalogue record for this book is
available from the British Library.

Redbeck Press acknowledges assistance
from Arts Council England, Yorkshire.

ANTHONY EDKINS
Haiku

Stealthily cats stalk
their imaginary prey
in placid gardens

CONTENTS

INTRODUCTION by BILL BROADY 11

DAISY ABEY
    Fynbos 13
SHAMIM AZAD
    Organic and non-organic cat 14
ELIZABETH BARTLETT
    Student as Cat Rumpler 15
    Scenes from an Urban Hothouse 16
    Dig 17
    Pushkin 19
MARTIN BATES
    Entertaining the Beast 20
CATHERINE BENSON
    To My Cat at the Door 22
    Fireman 23
GERARD BENSON
    The Scholar's Cat 24
    Minoushka 26
    Grace, Our Tabby-Blonde 27
NICHOLAS BIELBY
    Maisie 28
    Cat 30
ROY BLACKMAN
    Pippin Returned 31
GRAHAM BUCHAN
    Radio Pussycat 32
    Sentimental poem about my cat 34
    This Watch 36
JIM BURNS
    Killing Cats 37
    A Cat Called Bird 38
    Crazy Cat 39
PHILIP CALLOW
    Alone 40
    Cat 41
KEITH CHANDLER
    "Whiskers" 42

DEBJANI CHATTERJEE
    Praise Poem for the Cat 43
    A Winter's Morning in Timarpur 45
ANGELA COOKE
    For Jenny 46
    Night Visit 47
    My Cat Boldwood, A True Existentialist 48
CLARE CROSSMAN
    Anubis and Me 49
ELIZABETH DAVENPORT
    Purring Sonnet 50
JACK DEBNEY
    He Speaks to His Cats in Daft Voices 51
ALAN DENT
    Cat on a Cool Brick Gatepost 52
    Cat's Work 53
FRANK DICKINSON
    Death of a Cat – September 1939 55
    Chattan 56
    Felix Rouge 57
ALAN DIXON
    A Quarter of Cockles 58
    Ted 59
PAT EARNSHAW
    Is There Anybody There? 60
    Autumn Sunset 61
    Shells of Insects, Skeletons of Leaves 62
BARBARA ELLIS
    Statistics 64
SUSAN FEARN
    Night 66
MABEL FERRETT
    The Grumble-Puss 67
    Rogue-Cat 67
TERRY GIFFORD
    Death of a Cat 68
JIM GREENHALF
    Black Jake 69
    Kronenberg and the Cats 70
ZORINA ISHMAIL-BIBBY
    Cat 72
    Catdreams 72
    Biggle Puss, Maine Coon 73

MARGOT K. JUBY
    Astral Trip 74
    Tomcat 76
    Zamzam 77
URSULA KIERNAN
    Neighbours 78
    The Poet's Cat 79
    Edward the Transgressor 80
PAULINE KIRK
    Tippo the Time Lord 81
USHA KISHORE
    Benjy 82
    Gorrym, the Castle Cat 84
JOHN LUCAS
    A Seasonable Wish 85
ALEXIS LYKIARD
    Lost 86
    Found 87
    Mr. Cool 89
    Mouse 89
PETER MANNING
    Shadow 90
FAY CHIVERS MARSHALL
    Pledge 91
    Cat Five 92
    Rescue Cat 93
SUE PALMER
    Colin, the Cartwheeling Cat 94
CHRISTOPHER PILLING
    Mohair 96
JANE RAMSDEN
    The Real Mort (aka Black Jake) 97
SIMON RICHEY
    Cats 98
K.V. SKENE
    CAT
    can look at a king 101
    CAT
    and the fiddle 101
    CAT
    that ate the canary 102
    CAT
    curiouser and curiouser! 103

MARGARET SPEAK
     She-Cat 104
     The Tortoiseshell Cat 105
     My Cat 106
DIANA SYDER
     Cat and Penny Whistle 107
BARRY TEBB
     The Outer Darkness 108
DAVID TIPTON
     Thai Two 109
     Shut Me In The Attic With The Cats 110
SARA JANE TIPTON
     Fat Cat – The Junkie 111
MICHAEL TOLKIEN
     Without Tooth and Claw 113
JOSÉ WATANABE
     The Cat 114
ALAN WHITAKER
     Tabby and Ginger 115
DAN WYKE
     Found Poem 116
     Cat Stretching 117
DAVID GILL
     A Dog's-Eye View 118

EPILOGUE by JIM GREENHALF 120

CONTRIBUTORS' BIOGRAPHICAL NOTES 123

INTRODUCTION

Cat Kist – doggedly compiled by Jane Ramsden under the watchful eyes of Redbeck Press' eleven cats – triumphantly demonstrates that it is possible to celebrate the 'domestic tiger' without sentimentality or anthropomorphism. The cat in these poems symbolises political and sexual freedom, the familiar and the unknowable, the sacred and the profane but remains as Beverly Nichols might have said, 'just a silly old puss'.

Acknowledged poetic ailurophiles such as Alexis Lykiard, Jim Burns and Philip Callow are represented but there are new names too. One most memorable voice perhaps is that of Frank Dickinson, whose remarkable *Death of a Cat: September 1939* is a magical balance of the specific and the universal.

There's also a welcome emphasis on wit and zest in, for example, Graham Buchan's feline radio station that blasts out Shostakovich and Coltrane or the cheeky rear-gunning last note of David Gill's *Dog's Eye View* at the end of the book, followed by Jim Greenhalf's epilogue of allusions, *Reigning Cats, and Dogs*. He also immortalises Black Jake, the one remarkable animal (Mort – the tailless former elder of the Redbeck cat clan) who receives a double laudation.

Redbeck's prize-winning collections have been justly celebrated but this latest – by putting sheer quality ahead of considerations of inclusivity – is the best yet. However it is rumoured that even now, in David Tipton's lurid green kitchen, the eleven cats are stealthily compiling an anthology of human poetry... a manthology?

Bill Broady
September 2004

DAISY ABEY

Fynbos

Fynbos the honey cat
reigns over his territory.
A lion with flowing fur,
electric elegant
a rock, a king of hunters.
His night paws
soft as candy-floss
green-eyed lunar eclipse.
Blind owl's claws
a sharp wind
glaring through crevices into
his garden fortress.

In spite of the Persian line
a demon with rodents.
A tornado in a storm
a hissing bore-hole.
A vanishing rocket
a crashing Concorde
his mouth a trap shut tight
while he gently
rolls, curls and sleeps
on a sheep skin rug.

SHAMIM AZAD

Organic and non-organic cat

An organic cat eats chewed leftovers:
fish bones and rice
with a little curry sauce,
kept in a clay pot on the veranda,
and catches the speed of the wind
staying outside under pee-soaked sacks.
Its slim body is always busy hunting
in the barn and homestead
to combat hunger.

A non-organic cat eats supermarket products,
served and garnished on a plastic plate.
It gets Valentine's Day cards,
oversleeps
and suffers from high cholesterol.
It likes to wait alongside its human 'pet'
when its whiskers grow stiff
from potential threats.

ELIZABETH BARTLETT

Student as Cat Rumpler

Jean-Pierre Rumple, you call the bouncer,
And Jelly Roll Morton, the chocolate mousse,
Who forms himself into subservient
And unappealing shapes around your feet.
Rumpling is a form of stomach rubbing,
Bartokian, if done to music, brief
If done on the way to the long essay,
And the application form for a research grant.
Jean-Pierre offers himself for rumpling,
Fawn belly stretched in anticipation;
Jelly Roll is half-afraid, sometimes
Lies down as if to be a bouncer,
Changes his mind, and licks his paws.
Family jokes, ephemera, gone so soon,
Until student as cat rumpler
Is owned by another cat and passes
The message on,
Quia ego nominor leo.

Quia ego nominor leo: Because I am called lion.

Scenes from an Urban Hothouse
(For Bathsheba)

Swinging from the curtains
she puts out a paw
for a piece of cheese,
scolds and chatters madly, and
on the window sill sees
the monkey tricks of starlings
battling for bread on the lawn.

Perched on the radiator
in the bathroom she utters
her plangent and diverse crooning
and then crossly mutters
as the taps are turned off, mooning
at you with a woman or a child's
soft eyes, begs for a baby-ride.

Lying on the pillow, her long
black arms around my neck
she coils her tail around my wrist,
sleeps a little, then begins to wreck
the room with a quick hook and twist,
plucks out the sedges you brought
home from Cuckmere Haven.

Sitting up at table, she eats
with us, delicately nibbling rice
and spaghetti, luminous eyes
in a black face, grooms with nice
fastidiousness, jumps down and tips
up the garbage can, grows pensive,
imagines a house crowded with trees.

Asleep on the mantlepiece
we see her thin long tail
dangling like a jungle creeper
and the soft movement of her pale
chest fur. We, her keepers,
could not now ever leave her,
hooked as David on the Hittite's wife.

Dig

We had a cat once. We called him Pushkin.
A fine literary name we thought, and all
Our cats, Proust, Orlando, FitzWilliam
Turned into Prudie, Kitzer, Will, and so did he.
We called him Dig.
In our middle-age, we thought, a Siamese,
We had a bit more money, I'd never
Had one, we'd give ourselves a treat.
He came like a little wild fox,
Every day he ambushed our feet,
And ate and ate like a starving cat,
Ripping up the chairs with sharp claws,
Hanging round our necks like a feather boa,
Light as a feather, but faintly rough in the pelt
Like a dog, diggy dog, but soft on the head
And stomach like the finest creamy silk.
He flung himself on shelves and wardrobes,
And slid on the shiny lid of the desk, and rapscallion
Kitten, falling in the fish pond, returning home
Like a thin grey rat, drenched to the skin.
As he grew, his suede boots became long and slender,
The boisterous ways almost disappeared,
He became gentle, but regal, a Siamese prince,
We used to say, in spite of all the legends
Being a bit wrong, and we not used to princes
Of any kind.
He lay under the apple tree in the long grass.
We didn't cut it, and a small hollow formed
Where he lay watching the birds, but never catching one,
Those blue eyes were a bit short-sighted we thought,
Not functional. In the summers we got out the day bed,
Made for humans, but he made it his own,
lifting his head and sniffing the air, falling asleep
In the sun. The third summer was wonderful,
Everybody said so, days without rain and sun
To warm the bones.
At the end of that long hot summer he died,
Drooling from his mouth, his breathing
Stertorous, his eyes sunk in his head, the second eye-lid
Covering the brilliant blue.

We knew about such things. We read our cat books
Diligently, and we took him to the vet. We did all she said -
Miserable, distasteful things, forcing food into his mouth,
We cleaned his mouth and nose, and talked to him,
And in the end we lay with him the last day,
Stroking and talking, his front paws stiff with spittle,
Until he died.

Pushkin

No, don't make a mistake, he did not write.
He was just a writer's cat, who came
on an angel-visit, that delightful intercourse
of short duration. His literary name,
his stilted walk, his slight fawn body,
and his blue eyes staring from that strange
dark mask, those affected brown suede boots,
had the other cats, who didn't like change
of any kind, falling about laughing.

In their defence it has to be said
that many turned up in black fur
when word got round that he was dead.
Others wandered by in gold or grey,
with cobby peasant heads and legs,
padding across the mounded turf,
and urinated daily where he lay.

MARTIN BATES

Entertaining the Beast
(For Patch)

All cats aspire
to the lean and noble profile
of their ancestors.
We see it as they stretch and
nonchalantly yawning
reveal through a blast of Jellymeat Whiskas
shocking razor teeth.

As strange winds of dawn
bristle round the bungalows
the lean hunter returns,
profiled against the horned moon,
his eyes dark wells of memory.

But, like us, cats gets distracted
by those that love them.
They run to seed
or lose their gonads
to caution and prudence.

They bloat and roll into sagbags
tripping the slippered fool
who empties the ashtrays
or jumping on the beldame
as she stoops mid-cough.

Claws stuck in frayed cardigan
they hang there screeching
like swollen fruit
while the family eddies
between horror and laughter.

Like us also, their names reduce them
to pooch or fluff or bubbles.
Companion of the horned moon
dwindling to blend with the décor.

As I write now
my scraggy old cat revisits her kittenhood.
Chasing the scratch of pen on paper
she begins a dance to the sun-god.

She shoves my pen with a rumble
and scattering of fleas
rolls her warm tummy in bliss
but forgetting her fatness she rolls too far
and ends in a heap on the ground.

There's no knowing the dignity of a cat
even the lumpiest fleabag.
She affects disdain as mother blackbird
skitters dismayed in the hollybush.

When her eyes turn on you all is forgiven
although it may be only meat on her mind
- only meat!
Then it may be her eyes are calling you inwards
to play tigers in the jungle of her heart.

CATHERINE BENSON

To My Cat at the Door

Mouser
In and out the houser
Come purr on my lap.

Soft paw walker
Night-life stalker
Roof-top creeper
Garden wall leaper
Daytime sleeper
Come purr on my lap.

Ignore that midnight choir.
See how the fire
Embraces the air
Warming our chair.
Let the moon have the night,
Let other cats fight,
Come purr,
Purr on my lap.

Let the witch
On her hazel switch
Find a new familiar,
The year grows chillier
Come...
..........purr on my lap.

Fireman

She takes no pleasure in garden bonfires,
the cremation of autumn; feels horror
at a guy slumped in flames; is haunted
by an old smoulder in the leftover circles of ash -
stains on a November morning.
The old smoulder

of twenty-seven flat white beach stones,
perfect as she could find,
placed in her childhood garden.
Now white stones on a beach
skip 'ducks and drakes' across years;
tap out a morse mayday on water.

Between each dancing touch-down,
each haunting of ash, the slow burn of recall -
when he'd come home, face grim;
when she'd listened, unnoticed,
dressing her doll, rocking it to sleep;
the words branding.

Skeletons of cats, he'd said, cats of all ages,
they must have starved. Twenty-seven all told.
In corners. On shelves. In her mind forever.
And the old rag-and-bone man
'gone in the head', who didn't cool the ashes;
dead in his bed in his stable-yard hovel.

The old man who once gave her a windmill
that whirred tongues of red and yellow to orange,
who had only a handcart and kept cats.
The other man found in the blackened room:
in the other, where ashes had smouldered in newspaper packets,
the cats. The cats – shut up, starved, burnt.

GERARD BENSON

The Scholar's Cat

Pangur, my white cat, and I
We each a different skill apply;
His art is all in hunting mice,
Mine is in thought, deep and precise.

My greatest joy is just to sit
And con my page with subtle wit;
While Pangur Ban will frisk and play
Nor envy me my quieter way.

We are companions, never bored,
In our small house, in true accord
We test our faculties, and find
Some occupation for the mind.

He, by his arts, can trap and kill
A hapless mouse with perfect skill.
And I, after much careful gleaning,
Can bring to light a hidden meaning.

His eye, as keen as any sword,
Is focussed on the skirting board;
While I direct my milder looks
Upon the knowledge in my books.

When he pursues a mouse with speed,
Pangur rejoices in the deed;
I exult when in the brain
Some knotty point at last comes plain.

Though we are always thus together,
We neither one obstruct the other;
Pangur and I pursue alone
Two separate arts, to each his own.

His curious work is his delight,
Which he rehearses day and night
And daily I bring clarity
Where there had been obscurity.

*Metrically-correct translation of a 9th century Irish poem
(copyright Gerard Benson), believed to be the first poem ever to
mention a domestic cat.*

Minoushka

The leaves swirl in the wind,
Yellow and gold and brown,
And, brown and gold, Minou
Hunts them up and down,
A tiny frisking clown.

A whisking, frisking scrap,
She bends in the afternoon sun.
She tumbles after her leaf,
Choosing a particular one:
Pounce! And the game is done.

Then she slinks, a minute panther,
The leaf gripped in her jaws,
Across the October grass,
To fetch her trophy indoors
Padding on delicate paws.

Grace, Our Tabby-Blonde

Grace, our tabby-blonde, whose plump "murraoo!"
Conveyed such subtle shades of meaning
      Has left us now.
Of late beside the fire she'd socialise,
Stretching her claws, or, indolently preening,
      Blink her slow eyes.

Time was, her style of manners was less nice,
When tribute from the garden she would fetch
      Of headless mice
Or ravaged finch. Agent she was for Death,
Who now, without remorse, ungrateful wretch,
      has stopped her breath.

NICHOLAS BIELBY

Maisie
(For my daughter and her kitten)

Main-chance Maisie,
eyes wide as a daisy,
wild-eyed crazy,
all roister-doister,
joyful boister,
harum-scarum, couldn't carum,
anything darum
the world her oyster;
nothing could damp her
skitter and scamper;
a smidgeon of kitten
never shy (never bitten)
climbs leg or tree
indifferently -
needle claws in
without pausing
exploring places,
branches, faces,
always sure of
my and your love,
strokes and huggles,
tickles, snuggles -
then helter-skelter,
blitzer, belter,
tissue tamperer,
scamp and scamperer -
oh, to pamper her,
mash with a spoon a
dish of tuna,
watch her nuzzle
in her muzzle
and then guzzle
all the yummy
fish, in her tummy
tight and drummy,
and then her purring
like clockwork whirring,
cicadas churring.

Tortoiseshelly,
white on belly,
clean-cat smelly
brindled, smut-nosed,
to the utmost
life-enjoying, life-enhancing,
dancing, prancing,
stancing, advancing,
glancing, chancing,
abso-total-utely all entrancing,
all aquiver
like a shiver
of light asliver
on a river,
for what all life had got to give her.

And then one morning,
to come down yawning
as day was dawning,
to find her lying, stiff and cold,
who was hardly three months old.
Laid out cold, and that's that.
Curiosity killed the cat -

exploring, climbing on a shelf,
she'd pulled a tin down on herself,
a heavy tin of paint, that struck
her with incredible bad luck -
nothing to show, except the tin;
the injuries were all within.
A rag of staring fur: so dead,
there's little more to be said.

No more her licking,
skipping, ripping,
no more her pricking,
swerving, nerving,
topsy-turving,
no more her thrusting, busting,
hurling, burling,
and then her trusting sudden curling
on your lap and deep asleep.

She's deep asleep in her last sleep.
Tuck her down and bury her deep.

Cat

eight p.m.
on a chair
the cat

uncurls
sits up, stretches
a ripple like

water alive in a
garden hose flows up
him, he

yawns, raises
a soft paw
and softly

licks it
makes ready for
the night.

ROY BLACKMAN

Pippin Returned

Warm, the tongue between the worn, clenched teeth
but the limbs relaxed, tail curved up over her flank,
the lower forepaw spread out as a cushion for her jaw,
the way she slept, for fifteen banked-up summers, in the sun;
but the head tipped back now, one half-open eye
already blueing after the vein's injection,
our last due the only true immunity from pain.
I lift her carefully (why?) out of the carrying-box
while Jill is indoors and the children still at school,
set her down gently, ease the tongue back in
but, shutting the mouth, I have to feel again
the soft throat, jaw-ridge, bristly chin she most loved
me to rub, stretching up, eyes closed, and grinning.

But rearrange her neatly, each precision pad
which pricked its way between the washing-up
tucked in, and wrap the vibrant patchwork -
tortoiseshelled blacks and tans, tabby-patterned gingers,
whitenesses of fur, that gave such purring pleasure
to fondle – tight in a piece of old white sheet.
Put the floppy bundle in a new black plastic dustbin bag
and lay all in an empty freezer basket till her burial
below that largest rockery sarsen stone I shall engrave.
I leave the emptied box with lid thrown back in case they see it
and wonder, and dismayed, are too afraid to look.

GRAHAM BUCHAN

Radio Pussycat

If I was stinking,
absolutely stinking rich,
I'd buy myself a radio station
and broadcast from nation unto nation.
I'd fire the prattling,
self-regarding disc jockeys,
in fact I'd have them shot
(I'm rich now; I can do that)
and I'd re-employ
all the poor old has-beens
who were kicked out of Radio 3 –
those guys who always got the time wrong.
I'd have poets as presenters
and certified drunks
as hosts for the late night talk show.
There'd be no phone-ins,
except, perhaps, for people who had lost their pussycats.
I might have a radio psychiatrist
but he'd be lazier than Frazier,
and his sole advice to the hazier, and crazier,
would be 'Ditch him, get a life, or even better,
get a cat.'

And my station
Would not insist on the news, on the hour, every hour,
and we wouldn't give a f*** about the traffic.
In fact, I'd scrap the news
except, perhaps, for a specialist team of crack journalists
who would report on people
who had found their pussycats.

As owner I would dictate music policy,
such that Ambrose rubbed shoulders with Shostakovich
and Jeff Beck with John Coltrane,
and we'd play Isolde's Liebestod,
for those listeners still with their partners.

We'd broadcast to the Balkans
and transmit to Tasmania
all the good news about pussycats,
with their tails erect like aerials
and their little pink bottoms
which they manage to keep so clean.

Visitors to the station
would trip over food bowls and litter trays
and find cats copulating in the control room,
kittens in the cassette rack,
and a warm tabby on the turntable.

There'd be no audience surveys,
no focus groups,
no marketing,
and we wouldn't give a toss about the ratings.
(I'm rich, don't forget.)

We wouldn't carry commercials,
except, perhaps, for cat-flaps and flea collars,
but they'd get their airtime for free.
And in the wee small hours
the world would be enveloped with the sound of purring,
like radiation.

Sentimental poem about my cat

I brought you from the orphanage
run by the mad woman
who had so many cats
her husband left her.

You, your brothers, to choose from.
You purred so much as soon as I held you
that clinched it.

But Oh God.
Don't get a cat with a delicate stomach.
Was it vomit or pooh
that pile you left this morning
and why on the sofa
you furry bastard?

I suppose you've got another ten years.
(There's no point in new furniture,
the times I have to sponge it down).
I'll miss you.

Story:
When you were little
you went missing for thirty-six hours.
Frantic – I leafleted the neighbourhood
and embarrassed myself in shops.
I summoned strength finally
to tell myself
you're gone
I've lost him
he's gone.

Your tail.
You were stranded half-way down the sheer river wall
clinging to the top of a vertical pile
under an overhang
with the river rising, threatening to suck you away.
I called and you squeaked out.

No way down, or up.
Plastic milk crate,
long electrical lead
lowered down
steady!
Time it took.
Paw, tentative.
Incrementally fear ebbed
another paw
you hopped in
I pulled like mad.

Meeting a lost lover.
I clung till your ribs nearly broke
double rations
curfew.

You don't remember any of this,
you ungrateful little pig.
You're a cat. You bring in dead pigeons.
I clean them up.

A neighbour says
you've been killing rats.
Good on you my son!
But another says
you pissed on her table.

Is it love,
across the species divide?
Sweet recognition:
the slap of your flap
you head-butt my face
claws ouch!
purr.

This Watch

This watch
is a good watch.
It's a Swiss Eternamatic.
When I take it for repair
the man purrs with delight:
'I did my apprenticeship on these.'
It runs a little ahead, like a friend
making sure I get on with life.

The polished back of this watch
graced my father's arm,
a gift from my mother.
The original bracelet
snagged his hair.
It felt his pulse.
They ticked together
for six short years.

I've worn this watch
since I was a lad.
It's mechanical,
I think: it must wear out,
but we tick together,
eternamatic.

I almost lost this watch
rescuing the damn cat
from the river.
It cost fifty quid to dry it out.
I wondered for a while:
was the cat
worth more than my memories?

JIM BURNS

Killing Cats

When I was a child
I watched my father drown kittens
in an old bucket.
He held them under the water
until they stopped struggling.
"The best thing for them", he said.

Around the same time
I helped a friend take a stray cat
to the local police station,
where they had a special gas oven.
A sergeant placed the cat inside.
"They don't feel a thing", he said.

And not too long ago
I took our ageing ginger tom
to the local vet,
and held it down on a table
while he 'put it to sleep'.
"It was the kindest thing", he said.

Now, at home, I stroke a new cat,
and she purrs in response
and eats the food I give her.
But she doesn't trust me too much,
and who can blame her?
I could kill her with kindness.

A Cat Called Bird

We used to have a cat called Bird,
and everyone thought that was crazy,
calling a cat Bird, but it was
the right name for him. All the
young cats came round to watch Bird,
who was the smartest cat I've ever seen.
Bird could open doors with ease,
and the young cats picked up on that
and all day long and through the night
would be in and out of the rooms.
Bird would sit there, quietly,
and then think up a new trick,
so that the young cats suddenly
had to learn everything over again.
When Bird died we buried him
by the wall in the front garden,
and listened to the young cats wailing
and wondering what to do next.

Crazy Cat

"The fox was around again last night,"
she said, and I replied, "I know,
I looked out of the window and saw
the cat just sitting there, watching it.

It wasn't afraid and didn't seem to care
and the fox kept well away from it."
"Crazy cat, " she said, and I laughed,
and said, "But maybe the fox is smarter."

PHILIP CALLOW

Alone

I look by chance out of the kitchen window
and there it sits – no, squats, soft-balled paws
and sheathed claws tucked out of sight, under the
forsythia on the grass cut only yesterday.
It's grey and white, a young thing.
It stares back, straight at my face,
as if asking, 'What are you going to do?'
How neat! What a nice surprise!
Squatting there all compact, like something
carved in softest fur.

        I can't see any birds.
When I open the door and make reassuring noises
it keeps staring. Fear in its eyes.
Then it runs off.
That shouldn't matter. Such a pretty
thing, and just passing through.
Not a sad stray like that other one.
I wouldn't have wanted the responsibility of it.
It's a lone animal that comes and goes.
And so unflatteringly occupied
with its own business.

Cat

Just there,
Passionately faithless,
Swaying your pelt
You make shadow in the doorway
As if to tantalise me

But you're without desire or contour,
Wavering superbly, black smoke.
I'm a puzzle, a judder of vibrations
Up your sniffing monkey nose,
And then the charge ripples hot blood
In your twitchy snake tail.

The sparks fly from your fur invisibly.
Circling, approaching sideways
You show the glowing bulge of green beads
As your toes know the rough matting
Finely, like a dark dancer.

Fierce with appraisal you run
The river of your black body closer,
Haunches coiled for the leap.
The landing, soft as the dew wetting,
Prises open a wild flower mouth
To unlock rank breath, the meat.

KEITH CHANDLER

"Whiskers"

What was it – a child's black mitten dropped
at the side of the road? But your mews,
tiny, implorative; big green eyes; claws
pitoning my sleeve, made us pick you up.

"No cats" I said. But, banished to the shed
in a shoebox, secretly baptised (named
for a cat food advert) bottled, prammed
like a baby..."OK. Just for a week" I said.

So you entwined yourself, subtle as smoke,
into our lives. It is a companionship
suits us both. We let you warm our lap.
You let us tug your ears, tease, sometimes talk

Great Wisdom to. Your role is to amuse -
those pretzel shapes you make when you lick
your behind. You have the feline knack
of never lying down the same way twice.

Your day is spent sphinx-like or elongate
on the sunnier heights. At 8p.m., kittenish,
your eyes begin to widen, tail to twitch.
Cat flap bangs open. Whiskers is Out!

Not much to thank us for – flea-powdered, fed
out of tins, mostly ignored. But fresh each Spring,
with a side-plate of guts, your doorstep offering
of fieldmice, fledglings is devoutly laid.

Now you are getting old, a bit of a grouch.
There is grey in your fur. You sleep more, hate
what you're not used to. We begin to anticipate
how little we will miss you. And how much.

DEBJANI CHATTERJEE

Praise Poem for the Cat

All respect to the cat:
it is a canny shape-shifter,

a wizard of disguise
and impressive pedigree,
a familiar
pet that springs
sultry from the ashes
of its sabre-toothed ancestry.
A flying tackler,
pirate, raider and marauder,
invading where it pleases,
entering without a by-your-leave,
owning every place
its presence embellishes,
and always landing sure-footed
on the soft belly of innocence.

Nemesis of birds and rats,
its sharp claws are sheathed
within delicate paws. So pause
to observe the eyes
that spit strange fire,
the perfect fangs in delicate yawn,
the tantalising whiskers...
It is the tiger's aunt,
the banshee's sister.

Whittington's better half,
it is booted and belted
and ready for voyage
and visiting queens.
A creature of mysterious night,
slinking and stealing past,
it vanishes in a flicker,
leaving behind the ghost
of a grin, spreading
like runny marmalade.

An orchestra of cacophony,
it mewls, it screeches, it rasps,
it whispers and purrs its pleasure.
It's an owl-killer with serenades -
hey diddle diddler -
a traveller, a fiddler,
a sailor, a fisher,
a scratcher of posts,
a disarming charmer.
It arches its back and leaps,
padding, with instinctive grace
and power, along the catwalk.
It curls on cushions and laps, lapping
up milk and hogging the fireplace.

It is the Goddess Bast,
spiriting through time and space;
three times three its crafty lives
through many incarnations.

It is a canny shape-shifter.
All respect to the cat.

Bast: the ancient Egyptian cat goddess.

A Winter's Morning in Timarpur

The black and white cat snoozes in the play of light and shade
on the carport's tin roof, under the ancient mango tree;
tail twitching, it dreams of plump pigeon and tender blue tit.
The scent of a hilsa fish curry wafts from the kitchen window;
infiltrates its dream and teases it awake till it yawns and blinks.
A family of sparrows hop in the pomegranate tree:
twittering delight in the young green of its leaves,
they play among the orange of its buds.
Frenzied bees weave among white lemon flowers
and crimson frangipani fragrance the air.
High on a branch of the drumstick tree a tailor-bird's nest sways
in the November breeze, fresh with a hint of henna coolness.
The coral-stemmed white *shefali* flowers make *alpona* patterns
where they fall on the dew-damp grass.
The hibiscus still droops in prayer
to the early morning sun, its double petals
luscious red like much-kissed bridal lips.
A squirrel mother and child stir in their telephone-box nest
and milkmen balance heavy canisters on bicycle bars.
The roadside *chaiwalla* lights his charcoal fire *biri*
and the newsboy flings, with practised ease,
a rolled *Hindustan Times* to the third floor verandah.
Trucks and buses piled with raw produce and day labour
ply from the pastures of Punjab and Haryana;
they thunder down the Grand Trunk Road
and the black and white cat shadow boxes a Tiger Swallowtail
as a sleepy corner of Old Delhi stretches awake.

ANGELA COOKE

For Jenny

The cat mostly sleeps these days.
She was never gregarious. She never pretended
to like my friends. Two winters ago bronchitis
took her meow, left her only a small cracking sound.
Now I anticipate her wishes – In, Out, Drink, Food.

Her eyes range after me, perplexed by new weaknesses.
She slavers. Her bladder is erratic. I am annoyed
by her ageing. It points up my own fears about
infirmity and, since she has become less lovable,
I love her less. While she, living as she does
in this eternal moment, wonders why I am irritable.

I want her to die before I must witness
an even slower gathering-together of limbs
for the final jump onto my high double bed.

Night Visit

She called late, a woman I knew through the cats;
Hers – a basic Tom. Mine – a young flirt.
"I think it's yours," she said. "Hit and run."

She led me up the road, her hand under my elbow
like a relative at the funeral. We knelt in the dirt
beside the flat shape which was surely only
a cat's fur coat, but it was Zola. Zola without soul.

The woman wrapped the cat in an old jumper
while I dug the hole. Afterwards we drank coffee
in the kitchen. I kept straining my neck
looking out at the window ledge as if, by repeating
the act, I could magic the cat back again to where
she always was when the first light came.

The woman went home then. I don't know her name.

My Cat Boldwood, A True Existentialist

Do not despise or mock my cat, for he is a Creation.
A manifestation of God in all His Glorious Furriness.
In all His Most High Whiskeriness.

In a sense, God at His Most Perfect. For Boldwood, my cat,
is totally a Cat. He doesn't look on a tree
and suffer Nausea, like poor old Sartre.
Boldwood runs up the tree. And being wholly CAT,
he is not alienated from himself as you are.
Nor does he suffer bleak pride saying
"God is dead. I create myself."

True, he doesn't exist, doesn't stand out in the world
as you do, but he is beyond Good and Evil because of that.
He has none of your terror of freedom. He has it
and doesn't ponder over what he should do with it.

Boldwood is God investigating Himself in a sublimely
untroubled way. Don't you envy him? Boldwood, I mean.

And my cat loves me. Oh, I know you'll laugh.
"Cupboard love," you'll say. But I tell you
I see adoration in his eyes when I appear.
Where else would I find that?

Boldwood doesn't discuss Philosophy, Theology,
Psychology, Psychiatry or Politics.
For he has the secrets of the universe inside him.

CLARE CROSSMAN

Anubis and Me

They used to come at night, the cats.
Into the backyard under a January moon,
caterwauling their coven of courtship,
summoning souls, in the two o' clock dark.

With the cries of ghost children they would
scatter across gardens: alleywards,
shrieking, on a rasp of claws,
leaving as talismans, fur and rabbits' paws.

The dog's hair would rise and we'd make
our own ritual: a door opened quickly, a light turned on.
An ancient remedy, from an Almanac of Cats,
with a bucket of water, to cure howling at dawn.

In the morning they'd return, and stare from the wall top.
Luigi: Ear-Partly-Missing, and Boswell: Brown-Velvet-Eyes,
serene in the frost melt, and full of surprise.
Hoping for milk or perhaps a salmon tin

and waiting for sun dancing to begin.
The darkness a memory, a pointless superstition,
an old wives' tale grown longer in the telling.
"We were fishing on the quay that night

miles away from the warm house,
that was another gang from down the street,
not us. Not us." (As if butter never melted,
and one could not see through glass.)

*Anubis: in Egyptian mythology, Dog or Jackal God of the
Necroplis.*

ELIZABETH DAVENPORT

Purring Sonnet

Listen to the rhythm of the purring cat
Rise and fall, rise and fall, as if a hidden part
Strummed like a plectrum on the throbbing heart
Strings, thrumming, threading this and that

Of course, the stroking hand may well be what
Through time and trust and treats perfects the art
Of regulating purring's stop and start
And tuning feline/human social chat

Cats make this music for themselves when
We're not there so our mechanic role
Is not the major inspiration

Rather cat's sense of being there and then
Content, replete, and for the moment whole
Expressed in rasping respiration.

JACK DEBNEY

He Speaks to His Cats in Daft Voices

He speaks to his cats in daft voices,
A master of early dotage, clanging the tin
Of the foul stuff he feeds them on, chow call.
He plays all this in a frivolous mode.

When the cats have gorged and received his act
With the glum silence of a mid-week audience,
He recalls last night's rejuvenating lust,
The white bathrobe inching up on her flexed thigh.

It's then he dreams of beginning again, nostalgic for Egypt,
Even its boredom – that slow tease of expectancy. This time
He'll choose his own room: a pure cell against the sea with spy-hole
Shutters, typewriter, bottle, a redemptive message slid under the door.

Attending the present once more,
He watches his cats ache with their wicked teeth for bird-flesh;
A hopeless quest it seems, the way air taunts earth.
Yet, later, he spots the lazier beast climbing a tree, its plump
Marmalade flanks lapping the slim branch, daringly railed.

The target-bird is beyond reach still, perhaps for ever so.
But now the man assembles all his daft voices into one,
Burbles of poetry the brief visitor like the edge of a bird's wing,
Feels descend upon him this moral chow call, a raucous paraclete
That urges his cat to strike, even when – in striking – it should fall.

ALAN DENT

Cat on a Cool Brick Gatepost
(For Alexis Lykiard)

I know how he feels,
that moggy on the five o' clock cool stone,
watching the hot world turn,
content in cattishness he doesn't con.

He flicks his head at a sudden sound,
lets me walk by,
like a prince lets a pauper eat.

I'm gone.

He's trespassing,
loitering with black and white intent,
to loiter,
a sphinx's paw his squatter's right.

His tail's curled like comfort;
you'd think he'd peel,
or weigh more than the mortar.

Where are the cat police to move him on?

He drops unjolted to the tarmac,
cocks his tail like a cock,
slinks off sleekly.

I know how he feels,
as he sleeks off slinkily.

He'll flip his flap,
stretch and prowl;
there's food anyway,
and snoozing on the rug.

Late he'll trip out for a sniff,
I'll hear him rattling bottles,
as I doze like a cat,
replete,
dissatisfied.

Cat's Work

A pair of starlings jab their beaks into the lawn:
jab and look up,
jab and look up.
Three awkward steps.
These creatures are without grace.
Jab and this time a worm
from the soft wet ground.

Who's paying for this meal?
Who has property rights on these worms?

Comes the stalking black cat,
not my cat,
cat with a collar who belongs to itself,
slow, intent, black from nose to tail,
with a black sheen in the silver sun on the wet grass;
and gone, graceless and surviving,
the two nervous birds,
into the apple tree,
as if anyone can own a tree.

All that cat's work is prowling on my property,
pissing on my lawn,
shitting amongst my raspberries,
sheltering in my dishevelled shed.
He's heading for the dole queue.

I'm reading in the morning,
lazy as a cat,
glance and look up,
glance and look up.
This time a sweet morsel from the book's dense page.
I squeeze it as it wriggles in my beak.

Back come the starlings when the black cat's gone.
Jab and step,
jab, step and look up.

They're a bellyful of worms
I'm a brainful of words.
Those work-mad birds.
Me and the cat don't twitch a whisker.

Then appears the grey squirrel
safe on the thin fence edge.
The starlings scutter,
the cat's curled up in a corner cardboard box,
and I'm watching the acrobat,
leaping in my garden
as if he's mine,
as if anyone can own a squirrel,
as if grass belongs to anything but itself.

FRANK DICKINSON

Death of a Cat – September 1939

I remember the kerfuffle.
The grey cat scrabbling among
the iron wheels of Billy Nelson's
cream-brown trap clip-clopping
through Moorside's mellow dusk.

I recall the brass lamps hissing,
hunched Billy spitting and cursing
and flick-whipping his seven curs
to lope with the swaying pony-pace
urgent beneath the stars.

A rough committee formed,
recruited from the ARP it seemed.
Helmeted figures gathered and gawped
and a mangled grey cat glared – its
matted fur legs kicking wet red leaves about.

Sentence was passed.
The night-men crouched and whispered.
So strange. Here was only a cat dying,
mostly dead. Dad – resplendent -
stiffened, took charge, filled a bucket...

Chattan

A cat unfolds.
An interchange
of comprehension
shows me second best
as he walks nightly
through organic
intellect,
- and fallow understanding.

I know nothing
that he knows.
I think nothing
that he has not
thought of before.
I move no mountains
that are held
by his Mohammed.

I sprinkle
cat repellant...

He shits on it...

Felix Rouge

A red cat, sinuous
indolence, pads on velvet
paws past picture-windows
by a path my son made
crazy years ago.

The red cat knows.
Never hurries – never falters.
Watches as he stares to reel my anger in,
revels in my troubled thoughts
on flickering goldfish.

He steals to dusk's quiet hush.
Crouches at the purpled edge.
Mesmerises three fat fish all
as red as he; and as quick
within their piscine empathy.

Time and time again
until the last moon wanes.

ALAN DIXON

A Quarter of Cockles

I have a quarter of cockles to share
With old tabby Cedric, my tangled cat.
After each cockle I make him stare,
Look lively as so long before
He became a shadowy bag of sharp bone.

He tells me he wants to live forever
If there are cockles, not mind the comb
Any more than the vinegar, salt and pepper.
Tithonus was lonely. He had no pet.
Old scrap, I hope we can shrink together.

Ted

First name
still the best,
resisting change.
Fat snake
Teddylong.
Head-shaker
(no and yes).
No lapcat.
Leg-grabber
and biter through jeans
- reminder he's still
Teddus Terribilis.
Purr like a tractor.
Back legs
of a kangaroo.
Jam tart feet.
Glassy-eyed
seen from the side.
Pinetop Ted
against kitchen pine.
Drinks blood drained
from frozen leg.
Runs to the sound
of a carving knife.
Tamed by treats.
Tamest bribed.
Fat rattler twitching
rings on his tail.
Rumblesnake
another name.

PAT EARNSHAW

Is There Anybody There?

Alice was fascinated by the disposal of human excretions. When someone went to the lavatory she would slide neatly in as the door closed. Demure, yet intensely curious, she'd stand silently watching the procedure, so different from her own ritual of burial in my neighbour's well-manured rose-bed.

After the noisy turmoil of the flush she'd jump onto the rim of the pan and, head well down, scrutinise the still-rippling water as if she'd like to slide in, follow that burrow. One day she discovered the plughole of the bath, cat-size, and squatted comfortably over it, urinating.

Some people think animals are no more than animated skins deftly stuffed with insides by the taxidermist's hands. But the steady penetration of Alice's gaze could never be mistaken for glass eyes. It was unnerving...

I remember when one batch of kittens was about to be born. Her small frame bulged like a football, the surface skin quivering as tiny fists and heads struggled to align themselves for the exit. Ducking her head, her front feet impatient on the ground, she beamed the unmistakable message: *Stay!*...

The evening before she disappeared, she sat quite still for a long time, her green eyes fixed on me with the single-minded engrossment of a pre-verbal infant before its integrity is wrenched apart by conflicting pulls. I could feel the urgent concentration of her will but I was too preoccupied with trivialities to adjust to her wavelength. It was not only the hollowness of the air that separated us but the blankness of my perception.

I never saw her again, never knew what she wanted. Words unspoken, actions left unattended. The stare of her rock-pool eyes still haunts me.

Autumn Sunset

The yellow chestnut leaves glow like gold foil, illuminating the sunset. Pink and grey lights tangle, the grass becomes emerald, the leafy branches of the hawthorn tree are lit by red bunches of berries. The wind is rising to the sound of leaves clapping. It carries the voice of my neighbour's radio, talking:

A cat's sense of smell is almost supernatural. It has two hundred million odour receptors.

Their dog slavers at my shoulder, spraying aerosol droplets... The black cat is called Vince. He is sitting on top of the septic tank studying the openings of the maze of burrows among the laurel roots. The rabbits below can't see him.

At night a cat's eyesight is five times better than ours. Bright carpets at the back of its eyes act as reflectors. They glow like the red ends of cigarettes burning holes in the darkness....

In the blue twilight yellow blobs glow from the windows, birds cut the night with their singing. Indoors, the quality of light vascillates between grey and yellow. There is an air of hypnosis...

In complete darkness the cat's whiskers serve as radar. By interpreting slight changes of atmosphere, it can negotiate objects that are invisible.

Vince jumps in through the open window. His eyes are prehistoric. A grey mouse hangs from his mouth, twitching spasmodically. He puts the corpse down, licks it affectionately with his thorned tongue. My stroking hand reminds him of his mother, his throat rumbles, his tail lashes...He curls up on a cushion. He doesn't know the meaning of insomnia.

Cats spend two-thirds of their lives sleeping.

Shells of Insects, Skeletons of Leaves

A young child is dying. She says nothing except *Cat. Black cat.* She is past wanting the innuendos and falsity of words, the self-absorbed complexity of grief and tears, of human possession. She wants only the honesty, the simple familiarity of a creature that does not think or speak.

A friend who is involved with the Hospice movement has asked if Vince will visit her. He is not suggestible. I anticipate a stubborn tilt of the chin, and obstinate stiffening of limbs...

I have never seen him so gentle. He edges forward over the coverlet, stealthy, soft-footed, head projected forwards as if creeping up on a large butterfly he wants to investigate, make friends with. If he can get near enough without frightening it.

The child has sunk into the simplicity of senses. A cat is warmth, touch, nearness to something living, a comfort her pain can lean against. Vince stretches himself against her side, his nose under her chin, his fore paws on either side of her neck. The hushed regularity of his purrs has the feather-light precision of Bach played on a clavichord. His breath stirs her hair. Her breath is the mild quickening of air at dawn when birds announce their wakening. The two are bonded together, a depth of tenderness flows between them, cradling her last moments.

The stillness seems absolute, a unity deeper than consciousness as she falls into a light doze, passes to a deeper sleep, gives a slight gasp. The silent rise and fall of her chest falters, stops. The pallor of her hand against Vince's fur turns to a waxy lustre as blood withdraws from the veins leaving them colourless. He is a slack weight as I pick him up. Head, tail and feet dangle. There are too many bits of him...

On the grass he lies like a dead rabbit, extended. Only the faint movement of his abdomen shows he's alive. Shadows of silver birch skitter across him. The bright yellow of Hypericum flowers dance on an ink-stained sky. The trees toss with the long uneven whoosh of waves breaking.

Birds become curious, hop nearer. An approaching dog snuffles. Vince staggers to a sitting position. He sighs brokenly as if catching his breath, gives a huge yawn that almost dislocates his jaw, begins to wash his face, licking his paw and rubbing it forcefully over his whiskers, nose ears, right side left side, over and over, re-establishing his identity, smoothing his fur to make it more insulating.

Interrupted by some preoccupation he stops, his eyes vacant. The tip of his pink tongue stays poking out of his mouth.

BARBARA ELLIS

Statistics

This week I have been
wrestling with statistics.
Before I'd had time to assimilate
the shoebox and the thimble
metaphor – you know the one -
just one shoebox of ova could
repopulate the world
(although it never said what size)
and only a thimbleful of sperm
etc., thus rendering redundant
nearly all the men I know – and then
coming to terms with human genomes
and the recently published fact
that we have a mere 300 genes
more than an average mouse -
(which explains why Tabitha
bites me experimentally from
time to time, an understandable error)
now this – how one female
cat or queen
can in her lifetime bear
fifty thousand offspring.

I know cats are resourceful
as well as being randy, but
how can they find enough
places to drop a litter?
They could soon run out of options -
backs of airing cupboards,
lorry engines, the space between
tent roof and flysheet, ducks' nests,
old conduits, inaccessible
roofs where firemen scramble
to rescue apparently abandoned cats.

There will come a time when
every book you take from any shelf
reveals a mewling still-blind kitten -
opening the refrigerator door
will be fraught with possibilities,
cats thicker than coats, nurtured on
frozen pizza, huddled round
the light that never goes out now;
take care to keep the washing machine
closed at all times; and as for bed -
forget it!
That high tog duvet is just the thing
for whole communes of cats
rather like aristos' palaces
after the Revolution.

There is nothing for it -
Bolt the cat flap, lecture the cat
on the feline virtues
of chastity, or else
the threat of one last visit
to the Vet.

SUSAN FEARN

Night

When in the wild oblong
of the midnight garden
my cat plagues a mouse

not even the sadness and
purity of plainsong in
my lamplit room

keeps off the dark.

MABEL FERRETT

The Grumble-Puss

The Grumble-Puss, the Grumble-Puss
is always first to go,
no matter what the weather,
hail, rain or driving snow;
he wuffs his breakfast, cannot wait
to say Hello, Goodbye;
adventure calls and earthy smells,
the vast wide-open sky.

By teatime, sated, hungry, cold,
he thinks of food once more, of
kindly voices, the welcome of
an ever-open door.
You hear a rumble like the roar
of an approaching train -
it is the Grumble-Puss' purr
as he trots home again.

Rogue-Cat

I keep my mistress as a pet;
I could take leave of her, but yet
she was so generous from the start
that she and I will never part.

She feeds me liver, fish and meat.
My happiness is so complete
when she makes the bed each day,
at night I allow her too to stay.

I rule with such a tender paw
she scarcely feels the feline law
applied in manner Machiavellian -
"Cats never tolerate rebellion."

TERRY GIFFORD

Death of a Cat

She was ready to die, knew it was her time,
Stopped lapping at water held out before her.

> On lawns, lakes and low ground, white
> Winter mist cuts off trees at the roots.

Sixteen years ago she followed a divorce:
"Mum, now we can keep a cat!"

> Shrunk back into branches, still stems,
> The patience of trees diminishes us.

Whiskers a mile wide, she kept to the garden,
Failed to catch bird, mouse or butterfly.

> In boles and holes, under branches,
> White pupa keep the small birds alive.

Children fledged, mother away, she crept
Into her box in the garage to die.

> Night comes fingering through the fog
> And the fox unfurls for her dustbin patrol.

The weight of night's ice prunes the woods,
But the death of our pet diminishes us.

L. Cooper

JIM GREENHALF

Black Jake

With the shoulders of a Pamplona bull
and the stub of a tail
like a Chicago blackjack,
Jake the black cat fears nothing
on four legs, will even attack
bulldogs and run them off
their ugly bathtub legs.
Yet this Ernest Hemingway of cats
quivers behind the fridge
at the slightest crack
of rockets or whizzbangs
overhead. Like Hemingway's hero
in *The Sun Also Rises,* Jake
unfortunately lacks
the essential.
Does this make him difficult,
unobliging, anti-social? Not a scrap.
How else could Black Jake
share his domicile
with ten other cats?
Jake's the most amiable,
loving of chaps.

Kronenberg and the Cats

Before age and worry
creased his
papery features,
before beer
fattened his fast-bowler's belly,
he used to fancy himself
a cool cat,
a tom on heat,
pleasuring himself
in the cat houses of Lima,
a puma.

Now he's a grey panther
bossed by cats,
eleven mistresses
with whiskers.
His house of poetry
is now a cattery.
They promenade
on his green kitchen table,
or sit on top of the television
Sphinx-like, proprietary.
Or they snooze
under radiators,
on landings,
down in the cellar,
at the top of the stairs.
If the house had a belfry
cats would be there.
He used to take in tenants,
now he's got cats
to pay for.

Forty tins a week
plus veterinary bills.
The vet can afford
to holiday abroad -
Catalonia perhaps
or Katmandu.

They have taken over
his study and bedroom,
leaving him the attic
in which to cat-nap
and dream fitfully
of pussy.

ZORINA ISHMAIL-BIBBY

Cat

Cat, little sunset
In ochre, you dart
Tiger stripes of warmth
Tying yourself to me.
You flash by chasing
Tail, or pouncing
On pretend fly.
Your eyes amber
Love until sunshine
Of feeling penetrate
Warming cold centre
Deep within me.

Catdreams
(For Purrkins 1986 – 2002)

He sinks into seas
Of soft grass spiking
Over black fur, body
Tubular against
Dock leaves, dreaming
Of who knows what –
To catch large mice
Or lounge by the fire.

He is still and deep
In oceans of sleep
Far away from me
This hot afternoon,
Each breath so slight
He seems to court death
Cobwebbed under table
Curling little paws,

Sinking, sinking
To lodge in my heart.
He will always be
My gift of love.

Biggle Puss, Maine Coon

Biggle Puss, Biggy, Biggles
Of benign golden gaze,
Coat of many colours,
Jacob's, God-given.

You are green gold
Spirit of garden,
Blend, melt into trees,
Perfect camouflage
Sentinel guarding,
Overseeing territory
Invisible from wall.

You leap forward
Tail plumed high,
Bound toward us.
No lovers running
Towards each other
On beach (hack image)
Can be happier
Than we are now.

MARGOT K. JUBY

Astral Trip

Stretching the silver cord
to moonlit thinness
I ghosted through the darkened miles between us.

Intangible as night
I watched you sleeping -
an arm's length from you, hopelessly unreal.

Only the cat could feel my presence;
regal indifference
mirrored in its eyes.

I entered through the widened pupils:
I felt the little panic of the brain:
I felt the molten blood arouse me.

I crept to your bed,
a velvet shadow;
incarnate, and longing to touch you again.

The unfamiliar flesh
filtered my senses;
I wore the feline body like a glove.

I licked the salty night-sweat from you:
responding, you caressed me in your sleep -
I arched my spine to feel the fur-roots tingle.

Gently, so as not to wake you,
with ardent tooth and claw
I mauled you.

Then, curled up in your body warmth,
I purred beside you
for an hour or so.

When I departed, both of you were sleeping.
Cold as a ghost
I traced my silver thread.

The physical ache has abated now.
You write that you've been dreaming of me
and swear you'll have that bloody cat put down.

Tomcat
(For Moonshine)

A tiger sleeps in the heart of my cat
though being grey he seems ethereal.

His eyes rehearse the phases of the moon:
milky with love – or sharp for blood.

But how can that save him from being flayed,
from car-wheels and from vivisection?

His skin alone would fetch seven pounds fifty.
I keep him virtually prisoner.

So he goes prowling, prowling in his sleep,
incessantly dreaming of queens in oestrus.

His banshee howl is all frustration:
he sprays his limited boundaries.

I watch his elaborate killing games
with anything that moves.

Spider, mouse or cotton-reel
he taunts them with his spurious pity.

Being grey, he reminds me of you.
Tomorrow I will have the bastard neutered.

Zamzam

There are two cats in the house -
the old grey tiger and the new one,
the black one.

Who's only just beginning to look cat-shaped.
Her eyes are blue, but they change,
I'm told they change.

He licked her into shape, the grey one,
while she rooted around for a nipple.

She wasn't quite weaned when we brought her home
through the darkened park.
She buried her head in a sleeve.

We didn't expect her to live the night.

We called her Zamzam; not very apt,
being the Spring of Life in Mecca.

But she lived, that runt of the litter, she grew,
long after her unwanted siblings
were quietly put to sleep.

The old grey neuter looks at her with wonder.
He has relearned his kittenish games.

Two pairs of eyes regard our inanity:
the one pair large and owlish, yellow,
the other small and tenuously blue.

URSULA KIERNAN

Neighbours

Just recently two whippets came to live
in the small Sussex town
of Storrington.

The cats all vanished overnight.

Whippets have such sweet expressive eyes.
Such innocent and gentle natures.
Such tender delicate lines.

But where is Mrs. Randall's marmalade cat?

And the one which polishes its paws
outside the butcher's shop?

And the pair of ivory devils who make
those dissonant wails?

The whippets might perhaps have seen off
one cat or even two or three,
but for the entire feline population
to vanish overnight
without a trace or whisker,
this boggles the imagination.

As anybody who keeps whippets knows,
these dogs are biddable
and love to please their owners.

At times their oval brilliant eyes
seem to see inside our hearts.

Did they learn from us that it's OK
to do away with neighbours?

The Poet's Cat

I still catch glimpses of her disappearing upright tail.
And still see her polishing her white front paws
or stretched out on the bottom stair.
But there's no opening for cats
in mainstream poetry today.

Favourite cats are drowned in goldfish tubs,
unepitaphed, unmourned. Black cats,
white cats, tortoiseshells and tabbies -
all, all, have now been banished to
the glitzy, schmaltzy ghettoland
of calendars and greetings cards.

Anthropomorphism is bad. Where might it end
if we endowed the lowly and four-footed
friends which creep upon the ground
with any of the lofty thoughts
or deeply-felt emotions
which God meant only for mankind?

Yet animals feel love and separation-pain,
which might lead us to wonder
if they could possibly have souls.
Are we perhaps too tall to see
the beauty and integrity
of other kingdoms at our feet?

Diana sang me the Creation. She listened
to the words I wrote and patted them
as they came off the printer.
Then, when she took it in her head
to chase a leaf across the lawn,
this was pure poetry in motion.

Edward the Transgressor

What Edward does, he does advisedly –
Like leaving white hairs
On my dark clothes,
And dark hairs on my light.

How he yowls at the backdoor
Though we both know
It's raining hard outside.
He teeters on the threshold,
Thrashing his long tail,
Neither in nor out,
Until I don't know if I'm
Shaking more with rage or cold.

With a built-in sense of timing
He will bring up fur balls.
He will produce a partly-eaten mouse
Just as I carve the Sunday roast.

Although he has a scratching log
He much prefers our Dralon chairs
For sharpening his claws.
Of course, he only breaks
The best Crown Derby porcelain.
Then, when he's feeling
Extra full of *joie de vivre*
He'll spring onto my chest
And rub his bum across my face.

But I can never hold a grudge
When Edward rolls upon his back,
Presenting soft white belly-fur.
His golden eyes are lambent then;
Each claw is in its velvet glove.
Somehow I always give the brute
A kiss on his square pate
And yet one more clean slate.

PAULINE KIRK

Tippo the Time Lord

Tippo the Time Lord,
immaculately bibbed and pawed,
patrols our street, day in, day out.
At two a.m. he triggers our light
and enthroned on our step, surveys his domain.
Tippo is old, bold and cunning.
Your front door may be locked, the back barred,
but Tip is already asleep on your bed.
He will shrink thin and miaow to be fed,
when you know he has breakfasted on cream.

Tippo the Time Lord,
splendidly whiskered and clawed,
wears only the very best fur.
He's no ordinary Mog.
For thirteen years he has ruled our street,
awed rats, mice and visiting dogs.
Once, from his temple ledge,
Tip looked down on Pharaohs and Kings.
Now he judges us, knows every word.
Two eyes and a tail twitch near a hedge.

Tippo the Time Lord,
so well-dressed and assured,
has visited Memphis, held
passionate affairs in Acton.
What dark deeds passed before his eyes,
Tip has no intention of telling.
Rolling on our step, he accepts our favours,
then he is off – who can say where?
With broomsticks to ride, and armadas
to follow, a Time Lord's work is never done.

USHA KISHORE

Benjy
(For Susie)

You were not just another black cat.
You were *somecat* different: you were
a silver-tipped, greyish-black...
Was your name Benjamin or simply
Benjy? I don't know...
Between you and me, there was a bond -
the bond only possible between cat and
woman. Through those gold-green eyes of
yours, you told me of all your previous
lives: you told me you were a sphinx
reborn; you told me you were *Puss
in Boots;* you told me you were thrown
into a well, from where you found your
way to the nether-world; you told me
you were the palace cat who saved the
Queen from the fire-breathing mice.
You told me you were *Macavity the
Mystery Cat;* you told me you were the
Greymalkin that brought down Macbeth;
you told me you were Baba Yaga's
close, confidential cat; you told me you
were Dick Whittingham's personal cat -
And do you know? I believed
every blink of yours...
You were the emperor of all you saw:
You hissed at me; you rubbed against
my legs; you ate my lettuce; you soiled
my new tee-shirt and then apologised.
You jumped on my lap, much to your
owner's surprise; you purred in twenty
different tongues; you monopolised the
TV – But, best of all, you were a dreamer,
like me...

I remembered you in my letters and my
dreams – then they told me that you'd passed
away: I remember you telling me, during
one of our staring sessions, that this was
your tenth life...
On starry nights, I see you twinkling down
from Cat-Heaven – your gold-green eyes
urging me to dream on...

Baba Yaga: The witch in Russian folk tales.

Gorrym, the Castle Cat

Halt! Who goes there?

I am Gorrym, the Castle Cat!
I am Gorrym, the Dark One!
Come with me -
over the drawbridge, into yesterday.
I will take you on a tour of Rushen Castle,
through light and dark, where
great waves beat on the sands of time.

Stop here and listen!
A bishop's woe is written
in sighs on these walls.
There! A journalist's angst
echoes and re-echoes in the dungeons.
The truth within is trapped by the wheels of time.
I will tell you tales of treason,
of dire cruelty, and bravery beyond words.
I'll take you into the nights of time.
Here! Cannons blaze and gale winds blow.
I'll mew you stories of blood and gore,
of garrison rolls, of murder holes and
the hangman's noose.
I'll purr you joys of celebrations,
of banquets, wine and mead
of peacock feasts.

I am Gorrym, the Castle Cat!
I am Gorrym, the Dark One!
I count the chimes of the ancient clock.
I clink with the coins in the Mint.
I am mascot to the kings and lords of Mann.

I am Gorrym, the Castle Cat!
I am Gorrym, the Dark One!
I am the tour guide with a difference.
But when I hiss and my eyes flash fire,
stay away from me then,
for I guard dark secrets and
thunderous storms brew in my heart.

Gorrym: Manx for dark one

JOHN LUCAS

A Seasonable Wish

Pale belly to the sun, my old cat rolls
over and over on new-mown grass,
then stares up at a tree
whose blossom promises accustomed apples,
blinks and averts her head. No memory

I hope of how years past she'd choose her way
among high branches hurts her this spring day.

ALEXIS LYKIARD

Lost

The day you lost your cat you felt the mystery of pain.
You worried at the cruel word absence.
You scratched the surface of a nameless horror.
Needing some certainty, you searched inside and out,
wanting to know the worst that might have happened.
You were being played with, teased for lack of knowledge.
Not knowing was the worst thing: then,
suddenly you were willing to accept the worst.

The day you lost your cat you did not want to find
those other losses which had filled your life:
all that came back to you was what had happened.
Shock – when the best of friends was killed,
or the dawn of the morning when your mother died.
Numb dread – being betrayed by lovers,
quarrelling with soulmates to the point of no return.
Disbelief – abandoning your native land,
or when thieves drove away your worthless car.
Grief of that unreal day you stole a last look
at the house you were about to leave for ever.

Every moment you had loved, you now realised:
the sum of utmost pleasure, how
centuries slip away – such timeless treasure!
Can there be no goodbyes,
no coming home again?
Tears blur yet clear the eyes
and, looking in your mirror
you saw what you had lost.
Somewhere in the night a grey cat cries.

Found

1

Missing for three days now, she must be lost,
I told myself. The Devon landscape cold
and dark: a bark from dog or fox, a car
far off, was all one heard those winter nights.
The loneliness distorted all my thoughts,
froze them to fears like February frost
that clenched outside. I dreamed up accidents.
She'd been run over in a narrow lane;
lay trapped somewhere; a cornered rat or stoat
she'd rashly followed could have injured her.
Crawditch the drunken farmer down the road
disliked us both; I'd never know if he
were to dispose of her. His cruelty
I'd witnessed in the past. He hoarded land,
loved guns, hated the trespasser. Stray cat
would get short shrift... Then I played down my fears.
The nearest village was a mile away:
she might be in somebody's backyard, sick,
a feline felon gnawing tufts of grass,
having gone off for ordinary orts
but coughing fur-balls now. She had the sense
to make her way back, surely, casualty
or not? Yes, I'd soon see her with her tail
held high, friskily galloping across
the lawn and giving me her greeting cry -
a sort of prim squeak... But still nothing stirred
in the back garden. Opening the door
I tapped the usual summons yet again,
the spoon-on-saucer noise that never fails,
carries for miles over the starry fields.
The land stretched stiff and silent, as before.

2

The fridge hums and I seem to hear her purr
each time I go into the kitchen. How
I miss my small friend of the small hours, miss
her sphinxy crouch upon the cushions, or
the way she stares for hours into the fire;
the multitude of shapes she can adopt;
that jaunty tattoo – paws on wooden stairs;
her mischief mixed with joy when scampering.
At last a thud, the faintest scratch, and here
she is – perched on the kitchen window ledge,
pressed like a cardboard cut-out, flattened cat,
an anamorphic animal, quite squashed
against the misted glass. She looks so odd
I can't help laughing – mostly with relief
that she's alive to liven up my life
and has returned unhurt. Just a slight limp;
white paws and waistcoat grey with grime; sleek fur
a crusty mass of burrs, her whiskers blurred
with spiders' webs. The grubby prodigal,
let in, leaps blithely at my trouser leg,
reminding me she's hungry, she has been
out there exploring sex, an unknown land.
She purrs contentedly. I understand.

Mr. Cool

Cool, never putting a foot wrong,
making it, making pretty moves
and rarely caught off guard.
Fond of the lyrical improvisation,
a miracle the sweetness never cloys.
Sinuous, rhythmic, unexpected, svelte.
Neat mixture of the soft and hard;
the loner who can't quite belong,
won't always seek a cosy situation;
can rough it, loving luxury; is felt
to be tricky, laid back, lord of all the grooves.
Can dig, get high, has no less than four pads; will melt
you with a subtle music, an intoxication
like blues stirring the night. A personal voice
both soothes and sharpens. Feeling – spilt
into tough forms, appealing wildness in the song.
Relaxed, no underdog, the jazz-cat remains strong.

Mouse

Purposeful
cat

purr (puss full)

PETER MANNING

Shadow

Humphrey
has whiskers,
likes Whiskas,
eats Whiskas.
Not your adventurous cat.

Vinnie
likes biscuits,
'owt else, he won't risk it,
'cos he was brought up like that.
But –

Shadow,
though quiet,
has an Epicurean diet.
Any size of bird,
mouse or rabbit.

This week it's moles,
from their hills
and their holes,
that he kills with one swipe
force of habit.

Black-furred and green-eyed,
jaws sharp and wide,
this is the Devil's own spawn.
Eats them completely,
regurgitates so neatly

...at strategic points
...on the lawn.

FAY CHIVERS MARSHALL

Pledge
*(Winner of the Cotswold Writers' Circle Open Competition, 1994.
In memory of Bee Sweet.)*

You sprawl,
basking on the path,
a connoisseur of sun-warmed stone.

Time has hardly blinked
since you were a kitten,
ricocheting around the lawn;
thrilled
by a wind-driven leaf.

Your skittishness soon sobered down
to a dignified demeanour.
By day, affectionate companion,
graciously conferring equality.
By night, an unknown hunter
of the wild.
A graceful silhouette;
sculpture in fluent motion;
a warm armful.

Now an elderly gentleman,
stiff-gaited,
you doze away the days,
still trustful.
Trust me.

Trust me to observe due season;
to ensure
that you slip painlessly
to your last sleep.

Cat Five
('Planet of Love', Peace and Freedom Press, 2001)

last of the line...
resourceful self-rescue stray
edging into empty space

homeless, you commandeered
our garden, our porch,
inched into our home

gradually we fed you, groomed you,
took you to the vet
(snip not appreciated)

it was in your eyes
I first saw what hope
might look like

you rounded out,
coat glossy as a paint advert,
lost the wary glance over the shoulder

after scoffing food, any food, all food,
you got fussy, fancied only the best,
demanded entertainment

embattled warrior
playing like a kitten
with catnip mouse, twirled string

soon you demanded company,
attention, give unquestioning
adoration in return

now you demand our love –
but that you always had.

Rescue Cat
('Reigning Cats and Dogs', Peace and Freedom Press, 2002)

He came in out of the cold.
In a cat's 'Good Home Guide'
I think we might merit three stars:
* * * Meals: regular
Accommodation: comfortable
Access: own cat door
Grooming: daily
Attention: variable but benevolent
Seating arrangements: plenty of soft chairs and warm laps.

He makes himself at home,
develops his own routine:
leisurely wash, garden inspection;
semi-hibernation in winter.
He can tell the time to a 'T',
appearing by unerring instinct
when the fridge door opens;
defends his marked territory in tones of outrage
that can be heard the other end of the street.

he twitches in his dreams,
blinks and stretches;
and when he fully wakes,
he purrs.

SUE PALMER

Colin, the Cartwheeling Cat
(A poem for reading aloud, with relish!)

I
It is cosy and calm in the café,
Lots of customers taking a break -
Contentedly sipping their coffee
And carefully cutting their cake.

Then he comes! With a cry of "Caramba!"
He cartwheels in through the door,
He cartwheels up over the counter,
And cartwheels out over the floor!

The cakes fly in every direction,
The coffee cups tinkle and splash,
The customers all dive for cover
And the cakestand goes down with a crash!

Then the customers crouch in the corners
Till someone calls out, "What was that?"
And the cook finds his card on the counter:
"It was Colin, the cartwheeling cat."

II
It's a clear, cloudless day in the country,
The cows have been up since the dawn,
The cockerel's patrolling the farmyard,
And the combine is cutting the corn.

Then he comes! Crying "Catfish and custard!"
He catapults out of a train,
He cartwheels across forty acres,
Cuts a corner, and comes back again.

His passage is quite cataclysmic.
Catastrophe trails in his wake:
The cockerel goes catatonic,
The cows all just stand there and quake.

Then he's gone, and the dust cloud resettles
And the country folk call "What was that?"
And a cow finds his card on the combine:
"It was Colin, the cartwheeling cat."

III
"Hi there, world! Cape Canaveral calling"
The countdown is now underway -
Cantabria Ten's on the launch pad,
She's going to make history today.!"

Then he comes! Crying "Cats for the Cosmos!"
He cannonballs out of the sun:
He cartwheels up onto the nose-cone
And the countdown goes on...three, two, one...

It's zero – and yes, we have lift off!
The crowd roars with crazy applause...
And Cantabria climbs up with Colin
Clinging on by the skin of his claws!

They crash though the clouds to the heavens
Till the Earth's just a far-away place
And the crew watch with awe from the cockpit
As Colin cartwheels into space.

He cartwheels past comets and planets
Past Jupiter, Saturn and Mars -
He cartwheels across constellations,
He cartwheels out there...in the stars...

From the far distant ends of the cosmos,
To that creature that sat on the mat:
Is it merely a consonant calling?
Or Colin, the cartwheeling cat?

CHRISTOPHER PILLING

Mohair

There's a cat under the Renaissance chair. I know it's a cat but I made up the Renaissance chair. What I mean is: there is a chair but it could well be early Gothic. I don't know as much about chairs as I do about cats. The fur is angora, silky white with patches of light brown.

It doesn't want to come out from under the chair, even though it has no special affinity with chairs, Renaissance or early Gothic. Could there be a mouse in the vicinity? Or a mouse-hole? It is so still, you'd almost think it inanimate. An inanimate animal. I go to stroke it, braving possible hisses, bared teeth or claws. This cat has neither teeth nor claws. In fact, cat is hardly the word; it is a foot-muff. One you could stroke and it would purr.

JANE RAMSDEN

The Real Mort (aka Black Jake)
(Poem for David's 66th birthday)

Black Jake – "That bleeding hog!" -
is filching Feisty's food from her favourite spot.
Mort is also a Munchie addict,
not beneath begging for his 'hard tack'
by head-butting, or pushing his
tail-less, ball-less bum in your face.

A fur-fringed black-bottomed badger
bounding across surfaces, into Crunchie cupboards
and onto shelves, rear-end poised dangerously
until his beloved Brekkies' box is brought out –
though any brand will do
that 'maintains urinary tract health'.

Not that Mort needs any help in that department!
Pity the same cannot be said for this teeth.
But, after a Purrfect Omega ending to a Whiskas Complete day,
Mort still sends a great clump of grey Ghostie fur flying,
then retires – crunched out -
crowning Dave's head on his own pillow.

With Feisty at his feet, Kronenberg looks like an ancient knight.
He and Black Jake have been tilting at windmills all day.

SIMON RICHEY

Cats

I

I know only a small part of them, the part I can see. I see them through the aperture of my sight, which is the corridor they walk up and down in.

II

At night they bang in and out of the cat flap in quick succession. It makes me think of the pull that the night has on my daughter and her friends – only for them it is the lights, the music. For the cats it is the darkness – though they too come alive there, the same night running through them like electricity. At these moments I can follow them with my gaze to the end of the garden. Then they slip through a gap in the hedge, which is the hole in my understanding.

III

They are gone for the whole night. Sometimes, when I awake and hear them calling, or crying, or screeching, I try to imagine what it is they are doing. I think maybe that that part of them which I know falls around them like clothes and what is revealed, what comes into its own, is desire, appetite. Hunting, f***ing, raping. If I interrupted them in this, if I turned a light on them, I doubt they would know me. They would look up, straddled over their prey, and see no more than a stranger on the farthest horizon of their lives.

IV

In the morning they return, their coats smelling of cinders and garbage, the alcohol on their breath.

V

And ask to be fed. So I turn a fork around the inside of a tin while they step back into themselves (the tables and chairs resuming their familiar positions) their voices taking on again their plaintive, domestic note.

VI

After that they sleep for an hour or two and then drift around the flat. I will come into a room and find them sitting on a table, looking out the window, or lying under a radiator in a position of sleep, though without sleeping, only their eyes moving, or washing themselves on the sofa. They do only what they do. There is the action and them doing it and that is all.

VII

They don't live in time the way that we do, climbing into it each morning as we might into a boat, travelling the length of a day and then stepping out of it again in the evening, at night time. Rather they lie at the very bottom of the river, like a stone, and time runs over them and around them. All they know is the colour of the water above their heads and the way it darkens towards evening.

VIII

Sometimes we look into each others' eyes. Why have I been born into one kind of a body and they into another? Why have they been confined in this way, assigned less than me? What we have in common, for all that, is our occupancy of the same moment in time, in history, two quite different species ending up in the same place.

IX

Sometimes, when I go away, they seem to forget that I exist, or perhaps fall into a despair I can never be party to, so that when I return, and they see me standing at the far end of the garden in the pale suit I sometimes wear when I travel, the evening light falling, they run towards me ecstatically, as if I had risen from the dead.

X

The way their emotions have such a clear run of them; the way jealousy for instance can suddenly touch them with its massive voltage and throw them at one another without warning.

XI

When they fall asleep, curled up on the bedspread or the sofa, I imagine them drifting slowly to the bottom of themselves, coming to rest only a short distance from death, so that all that is left of them is the vacancy of their bodies and their hearts beating within them like something that has been left on.

K. V. SKENE

CAT
can look at a king

can outstare our pale posturing – Cat
plays along,
plays the fool,
plays so cool and clean mere butter
can't melt. Cat,
just by being cat, can see
without being seen – from a tree,
off a rooftop,
below stairs – lying low
behind that familiar grin
if
and when
it suits. Cat cruises the edge,
of our lives,
is in backyards,
      alleyways,
      off-hour streets. Cat,
you know us, you know animal
when you see it.

CAT
and the fiddle

With the lean and hungry look
of a cheetah in for the kill
you go for it,

greedy for prey (perhaps you've not been
loved enough) you show off, take
the careless old, gullible young,

fatuous foolish. You run
too fast, go too far
(perhaps you do not love enough)

for us to follow. Life
is a contest
between you and a god

whose name you've forgotten
and can't be bothered
to ask (perhaps
you cannot love enough).

CAT
that ate the canary

A sudden strangled song, sharp notes
clutter the carpet, leave a stutter
of yellow feathers on the tongue,
and that splinter of bird-bone
picking your teeth. You are full,

brim full of wings in the sun, gold
and green rainforests, blue
mirrors of lake reflecting
your eyes
at a distance – quite unforgiving.

We've been there, so often we've lost count
followed our heartbeat – only to swallow
the hearts of others. How soon
the music dies,
the party ends – for them.

CAT
curiouser and curiouser!

Through the window Cat
takes in the everyday,
decodes language,
  laughter,
  leches – one cat
can spill a mile of milk, scratch
long-distant secrets, identify
buried body parts (could
every cat-lover we know
be wrong?) We watch
Cat leave home, return, run
further, stay away longer
each time – just following
its bliss. Cat spies
with the eyes of a stranger,
lets the bird in its brain
fly
higher
and higher
  astonished.

CAT can look at a king and CAT that ate the canary were published by Peoples Poetry Letter, Vol. 3, No.5, Spring/Summer 1997 (Canada). CAT and the fiddle was published by Reach, Issue 98, March 2004.

MARGARET SPEAK

She-Cat

Our midnight tumbling
disturbs the cat,
sends her to seek
shelter in her basket.

My female shape
mirrors her body,
tail raised, back arched:
our faces deny the symmetry.

How like the cat I am!
Deep purr rises in my throat.
I wind myself round your body,
invite your stroke.

Sated, I stretch,
scent your musk in my pores,
tighten into my ammonite curl,
settle into the night.

The Tortoiseshell Cat

Skittles is everywhere:
hanging like a huge fur muff
over the arm of the settee
a red, black, white aureole

or an ammonite in her sheepskin sling.
The whorl of her curl
goes to her pink nose at its centre
and her upper paw is tilted

delicately over her closed eye,
while her tail drifts down lacily.
She is a fat bundle of pleasure
running now towards me with

a delayed chirrup, personalised for me,
and her dish of cream or pilchards.
Cat food is not on her list:
currently it is Cod in Butter Sauce.

Now she stalks blackbirds, or ducks
playing truant from Oggy's Pond.
It is all a game to her, the crouched
glittering intensity of the waiting

before the arched spring and the slightly
bemused expression as she misses.
She lurches out from beneath Forsythia,
stretches into a question mark loop,

elongates her mouth into a sabre yawn
and blinks deliciously, steps fastidiously
between daisies, inverts herself
and bicycles upside-down in sunlight.

She dreams Ichthyosaurus images,
follows spiders lazily along carpet edges.
As I said, she's everywhere,
but the snowdrops are quilting her grave.

My Cat

My cat's a hide-and-seek cat
but not a mild-and-meek cat
a certainly unique cat
and possibly quite rare.

My cat's a white-spot black cat
a tickle-on-her-stomach cat
a glad-when-we-are-back cat
she greets us with a stare.

My cat's a curl-up-on-my-knee cat
a doesn't-have-a-flea cat
a climb-up-in-the-tree cat.
Just anything she'll dare.

My cat's a loves-fish-diet cat
a very-fond-of-quiet cat
a doesn't-cause-a-riot cat,
at least while we're not there.

My cat's a scratchy-claw cat
hide-when-someone's-at-the-door cat
without-a-single-flaw cat,
a cat without compare.

DIANA SYDER

Cat and Penny Whistle

It never fails to set her
twining at my ankles
and purring in fifth gear,
the lightly up on the table,
nuzzling her solid little head
against my hands
and on hindlegs soft-patting
my mouth, cheek, chin.

This bad-tempered creature
turns all kitten drooly
and follows me eagerly
as if I might lead her
to some mouse-ridden place
where woolly jumpers are left
out by radiators all day long.

Oh, the places we might go
if I were not so stubbornly human,
if I were a door she could push against
to open and music were a way
of asking for something,
a way of breaking through.

BARRY TEBB

The Outer Darkness
(In memory of Blackie and Heathcliff, killed by the North London Branch of the Cats' Protection League, March 8th 1994)

When the day is bright and the sun
Flows into every corner of being
Lighting every leaf so its special shade
Shines and gives itself up as a shape
Of the shimmering jigsaw of creation,
Only then can I think of your deaths,
My loveliest of creatures, orphaned by madness
And driven by madness into the hands of evil.

In the night I was shown the ways of darkness,
How you were taken, my lovely ones, and hustled
Into the sheds of death and on the telephone
The abrupt veterinarian lied as he was told
And said you were diseased and when I asked
For the tests to be sent he fell silent.

I can and have learned to forgive much and often
At diverse hands but this was beyond forgiveness;
My loveliest of creatures, orphaned by madness
And driven by madness into the hands of evil.

DAVID TIPTON

Thai Two

A lilac Siamese, silvery white
with sepia tints and smudges of fawn
eyes like sapphires that glint red in the dark
he hunts birds in the garden but plays with those he captures
loves chicken giblets, strips of turkey
tinned pilchards in tomato sauce
shortcake if he can taste the butter
nibbles cheese and licks curry gravy
only eats cat food if there's nothing else.

He hates travelling in a car
wails the whole way, sheds fur and curls round the driver's neck
but settles quickly in a new environment
exploring each corner, nook and cranny, whiskers twitching,
        nose curled.

He curls up between us every night
complains loudly if we shout or argue
detests the click-clack of my typewriter
and certain numbers by Pink Floyd
sprawls out in the weirdest positions on the floor,
seeking warmth follows the sun from room to room
can't stand snow or rain disdainfully shaking his paw after each step
sometimes gazes for hours at television
and if feeling short of attention
jumps on the book or paper you're reading.

Stretched out before the electric fire
he's beautiful and spoilt,
prince among cats and probably knows it.

Shut Me In The Attic With The Cats

and preserve me from all do-gooders
lying politicians and media celebrities
who don't know their arseholes
                              from their mouths...

Shut me in the back bedroom with the cats
preserve me from ex-models and pop stars
celebrities and lying politicians
who write not only autobiographies
but lousy novels for the cash...

Shut me in the front room with the cats
half-a-dozen beers on the window seat
ash tray   cigarettes and lighter
                              sport on television
but preserve me from the commentators
and footballers who publish lousy novels
when their talent's in their feet...

Shut me in the bedroom with the cats
preserve me from radical feminists
                              and social workers
discussing rape or child abuse or drugs
from people who believe that they can cure
                              society's ills...

Shut me in the bathroom with the cats
preserve me from media panel groups
arguing about literature and the arts.
I prefer cleaning up the cat litter
in the cellar   shovelling their shit
honouring my presence by having one
probably thinking I'm their leader
as they accompany me to the loo
or sit on my desk showing no respect
for letters   bills   bank statements
                              or even manuscripts
so shut me in the attic with the cats...

SARA JANE TIPTON

Fat Cat – The Junkie

Fat Cat lives
in a basement flat
next to a pub
on the seafront.

Fat Cat drugs himself
on sun
lies beached
on the shingle
his black fur
bleached brunette.

When I greet him
a sun-stoned Fat Cat rolls
onto his back
offering the smokey fur
of his big belly.

Fat Cat has no tail
and only one ear.

One Saturday night
Fat Cat was beaten unconscious
by one of the local drunks.

He was found next morning
draped down the front door steps
his body limp and bloody.

Fat Cat was going to die.

Rose, the reformed belly dancer
had prayers said for him
at her bible readings.

Fat Cat pulled through.

Now he's always hungry.

I used to feed him tidbits
until Rose told me
the Truth:
Fat Cat is a diabetic junkie:
each morning his owner gives him
an intravenous shot
of insulin in his left paw.

MICHAEL TOLKIEN

Without Tooth and Claw

Going out for milk I notice slicks
of cat crap on grass and rockery
where small-hour yowling woke us
to murder. Finding no fur I blamed
piebald Thermal, so christened for his purr.
Neutered but not shorn of bully genes
he spat and growled at rivals half his size
till they shat their fear from lawn to rock and fled.

He'd pick on Stroker, little black
with a starry-cheeked smile. I've seen her
harried by blackbirds across two walls and over
a six-foot gate to land in splay-foot panic.

As for her po-faced stalker, my dream raptor
strikes just when he's unloaded where I've raked.
slinking off without a gesture of burial.

JOSÉ WATANABE

The Cat

I'm waiting for the return of the anonymous cat
        that crossed the ledge outside my window.
This ledge runs the length of several windows. And there's
no other way back. It will return
and this time it'll be more pleased to see me.

It passed arrogantly like some beautiful immortal. Cats are
unaware of the risks that the clumsy face
        in order not to stumble or fall.
They measure their steps precisely when they hunt or flee
        and never
never anticipate a mistake. So they create in our minds
their own myth.
And the pussycats of old ladies don't contradict this
because a cat is a cat, dignified and wild when the old lady
        sleeps.

Cats are dangerous for poetry, soon
they accumulate adjectives, provoke and seduce.
That's why I'm not waiting for the cat's return dispassionately,
so much beauty always makes me a bit perverse. So I tell
        myself:
it's fallen onto the pavement, lies motionless there,
        directing
towards my high window
                its last phosphorescent gaze.

ALAN WHITAKER

Tabby and Ginger

They slid your stiffened bodies
onto a rusted shovel,
laid you in a brown sack
still sweet with the smell of barley,
then took you to the railway yard
where the restless steam engine
waited to head north with the coal.

And, without a word or last look,
they consumed you in the firebox.

Poor rat-poisoned sister and brother,
not six months old,
released from the furnace,

white steam rising
in the clear sky.

DAN WYKE

Found Poem

Large male tabby:
white paws and chin,
fond of milk and fish.

He is a family cat
called Kurt
and is greatly missed.

Cat Stretching

This cat that I'm looking at regards me
through black pips in eyes like apples,
waterfalls down the wall, belly-crawls
through long glossy grass, and pounces
on leaf-shadow like a shoal of fish.

Then trots round daisies, back lowered,
legs pumping like pristine condition pistons,
each paw set down soft as sootfall before
another's lifted; slick purring engine
powered with more mechanical ease,

until something that shall remain a secret
tells it to stop – entirely, every movement
at the same time – and coil about itself
like a boa constrictor, trampling a nest
to settle into like a discarded pullover.

I watch it through squinting sleepiness,
feeling how I felt when a friend's mum
inched open a wardrobe for us to glimpse
a basketful of black socks rolled into balls -
except the floor breathed, the dark moved,

and had eyes that shone like polished coal
or nameless stars at the bottom of night.
Blinking back to today, there's a bowl
of flattened grass filled with sunlight,
and the clatter of twigs and wings

as blackbirds scatter from a nearby bush.
Sucking my lips, an Egyptian statuette
appears, dusting my shin with its tail.
Tonight I will hear mossy footsteps
pit-patting like rain on the tiles.

DAVID GILL

A Dog's-Eye View

I am sorry to poke my nose in here of all places.
You must think me an imposter, but please believe me
we are all cat lovers to a dog.

Here I feel like I've died
and gone to Doggy Heaven – a cornucopia of cats
all willing, smiling for once, inviting my touch. I've wasted
a lifetime on this dream.

Don't get me wrong, I could bite
a cat head clean off and would love to, if
I could catch one. But they have talons

specifically designed for soft wet organs
such as this nose of mine and I never bite
anything I haven't thoroughly snuffled first, except
in emergencies. So I keep my distance.

In cat company I've learned to pretend
I'm not really interested,
then they tolerate me, in time.

The closest I usually get to cat is to lap up
their scents as they pass, or wait until they leave
a place then plunge my snout in. They often catch me

rummaging through their leavings, but one thing a cat
won't attack is something that appears unconcerned about them.
I show them my big stupid face and they turn tail, voting
with their arses as they do. Unless their kits are about.
I have the scars.

Their pinched little ringpieces smell of kitchens and wet grass.
How I long to lick one. I've eaten their shit – it smells
like a dog's dinner, but believe me it tastes like crap.

A tom's balls smell surprisingly like mine, like puffball
mushrooms, only less piss, more spores. They rub them all over.

A she-cat's hole smells of honey and sea-salt. After a tom's
attention, it reeks of bleach, which I hate.

A cat's saliva smells sweaty and tastes of worms. I know
because a regular treat for me is to eat
their dinner after they've licked it. The spit
is the tastiest bit.

Tried some fur once but it stank of forks
and wouldn't blow away though I sneezed
and sneezed. Lost a night's dreams over that.

Cats broadcast their dreams, did you know? All
beasts feel them. Those with small fast beating hearts
dream darkness to blot them out.

Dogs of course relish the intimacy.

When cats deign to speak they speak
with their teeth and their tails. They keep
their knowledge in their eyes, which have no odour

like black ice. My tongue could unfreeze
their secrets.

They know I'm here. If they turned
on me I'd be dog-meat – literally.

But I know I'm safe.
I've never seen cats
co-operate.

EPILOGUE

Reigning Cats, and Dogs

In the guise of Old Possum, T. S. Eliot wrote his book of *Practical Cats* which the world knows better as the Andrew Lloyd Webber musical *Cats*. To my knowledge no-one has devoted either a volume of poetry or an entire stage musical to dogs. Walt Disney came closest with animated cartoons and movies such as *The Lady and the Tramp, One Hundred and One Dalmations, Greyfriars Bobby, Old Yeller, The Ugly Dachshund* and *The Wetback Hound*. We have also been treated to *One Hundred and Two Dalmatians*, starring Glenn Close as fashion house vamp Cruella DeVille.

Dogs also feature in a number of other films: *Beethoven, Turner and Hootch* and *The Hound of the Baskervilles*, to name but three. In the late 1950s and early 1960s British children were agape at the adventures of a mutt called *Rin Tin Tin*. In terms of celluloid, he proved to be the dog's bollocks. In the older world of literature however, cats dominate in a way that dogs do not.

The very first sentence that we learn affirms the hold of cats on our domestic affections. "The cat sat on the mat" – not the dog, the hamster or the pet mouse. This simple formation of single syllables is particularly apposite for the children of Beat poets and jazz musicians, for cats for whom, under the influence of the magic weed, the mat takes the form of a flying carpet.

Cats appear to be aware of their superior heritage. They stare at the modern world out of their pre-Christian past patiently waiting for us to pass into history. They are really rather good at giving the impression that we who look after them are merely servants. Dogs seek the democracy of a companionable friendship whereas cats welcome being made the object of special attention, yet manage to remain aloof when the mood suits them.

When Charles Baudelaire wanted to invoke the untameable feline sensuality of his mistress Jeanne Duval, he wrote:

"Viens, mon beau chat, sur mon coeur amoreux."

(Come, my beautiful cat, cover my eager heart.)

In Mikhail Bulgarov's novel, *The Master and Marguerita*, the Devil appears on the streets of post-revolutionary Moscow as stage magician Professor Woland. Among his anarchic companions is a large black cat which walks upright like Puss in Boots, talks and smokes cigars. Dylan Thomas titled his autobiography *Portrait of the Artist as a Young Dog*, but the earlier American poet Don Marquis paired a roach and an alleycat in *Archy and Mehitabel.* The former, once a great poet, is reincarnated as an insect but with his poet's soul. He hops about the keys of Mr. Marquis' rusty typewriter chronicling the tales of Mehitabel the cat, Freddy the rat, and other creatures who share the garage he inhabits. Lewis Carroll also knew something of the mysterious appeal of cats. The Cheshire Cat, its grin wide as a piano keyboard, has the ability to vanish and materialise at will. Its position in the bough of a tree reminds us that cats hate water but, unlike dogs, have no fear of heights.

When I was a boy I used to listen to British folksinger Elton Hayes sing about the Owl and the Pussycat leaving the world behind in their beautiful pea-green boat. I always thought *The Owl and the Pussycat* superior to Patti Page's sugary *How Much Is That Doggy In The Window?* A paucity of wit, but then some Americans do tend to sentimentalise their relationships with their dogs, from Red Foley's 1933 country song *Old Shep* (a German Shepherd named Hoover, poisoned by a neighbour) which Elvis Presley later recorded, to the Roy Rogers' classic *A Four-Legged Friend.* Mag Records have a whole series of albums about animals. The twelve *Dog Songs* include the Patti Page hit, plus The Everly Brothers' *Bird Dog*, Rufus Thomas' *Walkin' the Dog* (recorded by the Rolling Stones) and Big Mama Thornton's *Hound Dog.*

Among the dozen numbers on *Cat Songs* are Norma Tanega's hit *Walkin' My Cat Named Dog*, Laura Nyro's *Cat Song*, Peggy Lee's brilliant *The Siamese Cat Song* from *The Lady and the Tramp*, and Tom Jones' ebullient *What's New, Pussycat?* from the comedy film starring Peter Sellers, Peter O'Toole and Ursula Andress. As I have returned to the movies I should just like to say that, in the world of films, hot dogs have not had it all their own way. *Cat People, Cat On A Hot Tin Roof* and *Cat Ballou* are just three cool cats of thirteen to match the doggy titles.

Dr. Samuel Johnson was a cat man. A fat pile of fur and paws called Hodge – "a very fine cat indeed" – shared his various Fleet Street lodgings. The Lord Mayor of London, Dick Whittington owed his destiny to a cat who, according to legend, commanded Dick to "turn again". If at first you don't succeed, ask a cat for advice. "Truth's a dog that must to kennel", observes the Fool in *King Lear*, whereas a cat will always tell the truth. When Shakespeare wanted to send up the Elizabethan constabulary in *Much Ado About Nothing*, he invented a character called Dogberry. Think of some of the epithets we extrapolate from 'dog':

dogmatic, dog-earred, dog's life, gone to the dogs, dog-eat-dog, dog's dinner.

The word 'cat' on the other hand carries a multitude of far more interesting nouns and adjectives: cataclysm, catamite, catalepsy, catamaran, catacomb, catastasis, catamountain, Catalan. Not forgetting the great Romans Cato and Catullus.

If anyone remains in doubt about the relative merits of cats and dogs may I remind them of the unassailable position that the average cat holds in the minds and hearts of writers. When T. S. Eliot described the Mystery Cat Macavity as the "Napoleon of Crime", he was repeating a phrase from his beloved Sherlock Holmes' stories of Conan Doyle. Holmes tells Watson that most of London's organised crime flows from the network of Dr. Moriarty, the veritable "Napoleon of Crime". D. H. Lawrence, arguably as good a poet as a novelist, perfected his unfettered line in poems such as *Snake* and *Mountain Lion*. In 1956 Sylvia Plath wrote a poem called *Ella Manson and Her Eleven Cats*. Not to be outdone, her husband Ted Hughes included in his 1960 volume *Lupercal* a poem called *Esther's Tomcat*. Hughes was Lawrence's true heir in the field of animal poetry; *Jaguar* and *Second Look at a Jaguar* demonstrate the hypnotic hold on the poetic imagination of cats, large and small.

Jim Greenhalf
Bradford, February 2004

CONTRIBUTORS' BIOGRAPHICAL NOTES,
with appropriate acknowledgements

Daisy Abey *(Fynbos)*

Daisy Abey, Sutton, Surrey. Born in Sri Lanka. Collections include *Under Any Sky, In Exile, Silent Protest*. Novel, *Like the Wind*, based on an immigrant's experience.

Shamim Azad *(Organic and non-organic cat)*

Born in Bangladesh, Poet in Education for Apples and Snakes, Shamin Azad received the Bichitra Award from Bangladesh in 1994 and a Year of the Artist 2000 Award for poetry from London Arts.

Her poems have been included in *The Redbeck Anthology of British South Asian Poetry, Mother Tongues*, and *My Birth Was Not In Vain*. She wrote *The Raft* and co-wrote *Hopscotch Ghost* for the Half Moon Theatre Company. Other compilations and translations are *Voyages from Bangladeshi Writers* and *The Life of Mr. Aziz in Britain*.

Shamin is also a freelance journalist who writes regularly for Bengali newspapers and magazines in Britain, Bangladesh and the USA. Her web address is www.shamimazad.com

Elizabeth Bartlett *(Student as Cat Rumpler; Scenes from an Urban Hothouse; Dig; Pushkin)*

Elizabeth Bartlett, born in 1924, grew up in Kent and now lives in Burgess Hill, West Sussex. *Scenes from an Urban Hothouse* and *Pushkin* appeared in *Appetites of Love* (Bloodaxe, 2001), her first new collection since her major retrospective book *Two Women Dancing: New and Selected Poems* (Bloodaxe, 1995, Cholmondely Award), which drew on more than 50 years of writing and was a Poetry Book Society Recommendation. Her eighth collection *Mrs. Perkins and Oedipus*, also from Bloodaxe, was published on her 80th birthday, 28 April 2004.

Martin Bates *(Entertaining the Beast)*

Bates being an anagram of 'beast', Martin lives with various ageing animals including 2 cats, 2 geese and a dog, but a youthful wife, 2 daughters and a son. He has travelled a lot while writing coursebooks in English as a foreign language. Nowadays he goes round in ever-decreasing circles out of which poems sometimes fly at a tangent.

Catherine Benson *(To My Cat at the Door; Fireman)*

Catherine Benson has been owned by many cats. She was born in Bradford but brought up in Scotland with her first owner, Fluffy. Since then she has lived here and there, and almost always with cats. She writes, has poems in many anthologies, does workshops in schools and illustrates as page twelve in this anthology.

Gerard Benson *(The Scholar's Cat; Minoushka; Grace, Our Tabby-Blonde)*

London-born Gerard Benson now lives in Bradford, Yorkshire. He is co-founder, co-editor of *Poems on the Underground*; has written collections for children and adults; and edited two ground-breaking Puffin anthologies for children. He has poems in over a hundred anthologies. His collection, *To Catch an Elephant*, illustrated by his wife, Cathy, was nominated for the CLPE Children's Poetry Award.

Nicholas Bielby *(Maisie; Cat)*

Nicholas Bielby retired from teaching at Leeds University a few years ago and is now editor of *Pennine Platform* poetry magazine. In addition to academic books, he has published two collections of poetry and won prizes in many competitions including New Poetry and Arvon International. He likes painting, sailing and making things, but most he likes entertaining his three granddaughters.

Roy Blackman *(Pippin Returned)*

Roy Blackman (1943 – 2002) was a scientist with a degree in Geology and Zoology from Bristol University, a Ph.D. from the University of Newcastle, and later, a first class honours degree in Humanities from the Open University. He worked for twenty-one years as a scientific civil servant in marine pollution protection for the Ministry of Agriculture and Fisheries. In 1991 he founded Smiths Knoll with his friend, Michael Laskey, and they co-edited it (Issues 1 – 30) until his death. A Hawthornden Fellow in 1993, he published his first collection *As Lords Expected* (Rockingham Press) in 1996. A further pamphlet of his work – *The Waterman* – was published by Smiths Knoll in November 2003. (*Pippin Returned* first appeared in *SlowDancer No. 24* (1990) and later in Roy's first collection, *As Lords Expected*.)

Bill Broady *(Introduction)*
Bill Broady was educated in York and London. A former croupier, care worker and cartographer, he is currently an Assistant Editor of Redbeck Press and lives in West Yorkshire. He is author of a highly-acclaimed debut novel, *Swimmer*, and a wonderfully sharp collection of short stories under the title *In This Block There Lives A Slag*. Both are now available in paperback from Flamingo.

Graham Buchan *(Radio Pussycat; Sentimental poem about my cat; This Watch)*
Graham Buchan graduated as a Chemical Engineer but has spent his life in the film, television and video industries. He lives in London with his wife, daughter and cat, Dumpling, who now sleeps at least 18 hours a day. He has published short stories, poetry, travel and film appreciation.

Jim Burns *(Killing Cats; A Cat Called Bird; Crazy Cat)*
Jim Burns, who now lives in Cheshire, has been active as a writer for over 40 years. He has had four books of poetry published by Redbeck Press, the most recent of which is *Take It Easy* (2003). Also, in 2001, Nottingham Trent published a collection of essays: *Beats, Bohemians and Intellectuals*.

Philip Callow *(Alone; Cat)*
Philip Callow was born in Birmingham and grew up in Coventry. At 15 he went into a factory as an apprentice toolmaker, then was a night telephonist, clerk, teacher, finally a full-time writer after receiving one of the first Arts' Council bursaries. As well as novels, he has published ten collections of poetry and five biographies. The poem *Alone* came from *Fires in October* (1994); *Cat* from his selected poems, *Testimonies* (2000). His memoir, *Passage from Home*, came out in 2002 and a book on Lawrence's final decade, *Body of Truth*, in Chicago (May 2003). His latest book of poems, *Soul Country*, is being published by Shoestring Press this year.

Keith Chandler *("Whiskers")*
Keith Chandler, a schoolteacher for 30 years, has been narrowly published and broadcast, including three books of poetry and a play for television. He shares a house with the grumpiest cat in Norfolk, now over 20 years of age.

Debjani Chatterjee *(Praise Poem for the Cat; A Winter's Morning in Timarpur)*

Debjani Chatterjee is one of Britain's best-known South Asian writers. Born in India, she has also lived in Japan, Bangladesh, Hong Kong, Egypt and Britain. She writes for both children and adults, having had well over 30 books of prose, poetry and translation published. Redbeck Press published her award-winning *Redbeck Anthology of British South Asian Poetry* and *Generations of Ghazals.* Latest publications are *Namaskar: New and Selected Poems* (Redbeck, October 2004) and a multilingual play for children, *The Honoured Guest* (Faber). Debjani chairs the National Association of Writers in Education and was awarded an honorary doctorate by Sheffield Hallam University. She has a web site at http://mysite.freeserve.com/DebjaniChatterjee

Angela Cooke *(For Jenny; Night Visit; My Cat Boldwood, A True Existentialist)*

Angela Cooke has two children and two cats. She works in Ceramics and as a tutor in Creative Writing. Her first poetry collection was published by Tarantula.

Linda Cooper *(Artist Illustration of Gemma)*

Linda Cooper did this oil on prepared paper of Gemma, the subject of Terry Gifford's *Death of a Cat* in 1994. The painting was photographed by Gill Rand and is entitled 'Please – take me too!'

Clare Crossman *(Anubis and Me)*

Clare Crossman was joint winner of the Redbeck Competition in 1996 with a collection called *Landscapes.* A poem from that collection, *A Lichened Tree*, was in the short poem film about the Lake District called *In The Mind Of Man* (Northern Arts, Nick May, for the Newhale Theatre, Keswick). Her second collection, *Going Back*, is from Firewater Press, Cambridge, (2002).

Elizabeth Davenport *(Purring Sonnet)*

Elizabeth Davenport is the daughter of Scottish poet and novelist Janet Caird. She has engaged in poetry in various ways all her life and currently writes it when she can't sleep. Her poem was a model for her husband Michael during his first attempts at verse composition. His speciality is terrible punning, e.g. cat*kin* – a relative cat; cate*gory* – a cat covered in blood; cater*pillar* – a supportive cat.

Jack Debney *(He Speaks to His Cats in Daft Voices)*

Jack Debney, brought up in Grimsby and now living in Germany, has published stories in many magazines over the years. Redbeck Press published a selection, *The Crocodile's Head,* in 2002. The poem included here is from his collection *Clowns and Puritans* (White Adder Press, 1999).

Alan Dent *(Cat on a Cool Brick Gatepost; Cat's Work)*

Alan Dent is the founder and editor of The Penniless Press. He has published three collections with Redbeck: *Bedtime Story, Antidotes to Optimism* and *Corker.* This year his long poem, *Memoria Technica*, has been published by Shoestring Press.

Frank Dickinson *(Death of a Cat – September 1939; Chattan; Felix Rouge)*

Frank Dickinson was born in Bradford in 1929, where he has lived all his life apart from National Service in the Middle East. He has held several different jobs, including as a fireman with the LNER, but eventually joined the Police Force where he served for Bradford and West Yorkshire for 31 years. His first full collection of poetry, *In Blue and Khaki*, has now been published by Redbeck Press, September 2004.

Alan Dixon *(A Quarter of Cockles; Ted)*

Alan Dixon's first collection of poetry was *Snails and Reliquaries* by Fortune Press in 1964. By his own admission he has been around a long time! He has had another collection, *Transports*, previously published by Redbeck Press and various in-between by Poet and Printer and submissions in many magazines – *TLS, Poetry* (Chicago), *The Listener, New Statesman, The Observer, The Spectator, London Review* and *The Scotsman* – to name but some in an exhaustive list. Alan Dixon lives in Eastbourne and is a keen cyclist.

Pat Earnshaw *(Is There Anybody There?; Autumn Sunset; Shells of Insects, Skeletons of Leaves)*

A biology graduate and former authority on antique laces, has loved writing since childhood. Her collection of prose poems, *My Cat Vince*, won first prize in the Scintilla Open Poetry Competition 2000. Redbeck Press published a 32-page pamphlet, *The Golden Hinde*, in Spring 2002. Pat was awarded a South East Arts Council Grant in the same year.

Vince belonged to the late Sir Harry Secombe and his wife Myra. Now getting on in years, he has a few white hairs but remains slim, elegant and charismatic. See **Sally Michel**, *below.*

Anthony Edkins (Haiku)
Apart from 12 years in Spain and the USA, Anthony Edkins has lived in London since 1950. His literary output has been divided between translating from Spanish poetry and his own writing. His most recent volume of poems is *Life As It Comes* (Redbeck Press, 2002).

Barbara Ellis *(Statistics)*
Barbara Ellis has lived in Dorset all her adult life and is married with two children and numerous grandchildren. She is a member of East Street Poets and has published five pamphlets, the latest being *'The Birds', Mass and Other Poems*. She has been frequently published in magazines such as *Tears in the Fence, Fire, Envoi, South, Sepia, Iota* and *Poetry Monthly*.

Susan Fearn *(Night)*
Susan Fearn has had poems and short prose texts published in many literary journals including *Fire, Oasis, Tears in the Fence, Smiths Knoll* etc. She also works with visual artists. Solo publications are *Marking Time, Relics, Sixteen Poems* and *Songs from the Piano Book*. She completed a course in advanced writing with the Open College of the Arts, which was made possible by a Creative Ambition Award from West Midlands Arts.

Mabel Ferrett *(The Grumble-Puss; Rogue-Cat)*
Born in 1917, Mabel Ferrett's published works include her major poetry collection, *Scathed Earth* (University of Salzburg, 1996), six smaller collections and a poetry tape shared with Ian Emberson. Other published works are an historical novel, *The Angry Men* (E.J. Arnold & Son, Leeds, 1965 – serialised by Olive Shapley and broadcast on Radio 4 in 1967 and 1968), *The Taylors of the Red House* (Kirklees Libraries, Museums and Arts, 1987), *The Brontes of Spen Valley* (Hub Publications, 1978, and Kirklees Cultural Services, 1992) and *After Passchendale, An Autobiography* (Fighting Cock Press, York).

Terry Gifford *(Death of a Cat)*

Terry Gifford lives in Sheffield, now without a cat. Very recently retired, he was Reader in Literature and Environment at the University of Leeds. He has written books of eco-criticism and six books of poetry including *The Unreliable Mushrooms: New and Selected Poems* (Redbeck Press, 2003).

David Gill *(A Dog's-Eye View)*

David Gill is a researcher and part-time lecturer in Stylistics at the University of Huddersfield. He devotes his life to spiritual improvement and hopes to be reborn as a dog. *The Amateur Yorksherman*, his first collection of poetry, was published by Redbeck Press in 2002.

Jim Greenhalf *(Black Jake; Kronenberg and the Cats)*

Jim Greenhalf has lived and worked as a writer in Bradford for nearly 30 years. He is the author of the best-selling *Salt and Silver: A Story of Hope* and *It's A Mean Old Scene: A History of Bradford since 1974*, as well as a selection of short stories, *Father Jim* (Redbeck Press, 2002). Redbeck Press has also published four collections of his poetry: *The Dog's Not Laughing* (1999), *Following the Seine* (2000), *The Unlikelihood of Intimacy in the Next Six Hours* (2001) and *In the Hinterland* (2003).

Zorina Ismail-Bibby *(Cat; Catdreams; Biggle Puss, Maine Coon)*

Zorina Ismail-Bibby is originally from Guyana in tropical South America. She migrated to Britain in the 1960s but was brought up in the country surrounded by wildlife and pets (including cats of course!). Today she still particularly enjoys animals as subjects for her paintings. Zorina was County Coordinator for ESOL and later a lecturer at Northampton College. A keen environmentalist, she is a founder member of St. George's Community and Wildlife Group in Northampton, where she also facilitates the Chameleon Writers' Cooperative. Zorina's short stories and poems have won various prizes, been widely published and also broadcast on radio. A poetry collection, *After a Cold Season – Rising*, was published in 1988. In 1994 she was awarded an East Midlands' Arts Bursary to complete her novel, *The Outcasts: Corentyne Scandal.*

Margot K. Juby *(Astral Trip; Tomcat; Zamzam)*

Margot K. Juby was born in King's Lynn, Norfolk. She read English at Hull University, graduating with first-class honours, and has lived in Hull (with increasing reluctance) ever since. A veteran of small presses, appearances in print have included *Tribune, The Scotsman, Bête Noire, The Rialto, The Wide Skirt, Iron* and more, plus TV and radio. She is the only 'new poet from Hull' (Bloodaxe, 1982) who was also 'a writer of East Anglia' (Secker and Warburg, 1977). Her fourth booklet, *The Tactful Foetus* (Sol Publications) was published in 1995. Her three previous publications are collected in *Triple Whammy* (Braquemard, 1996). Her latest publication, *Erl-King's Bride*, was recently produced by Moonshine Press. *Tomcat* has been previously published in *The Bad Seed Review*.

Ursula Kiernan *(Neighbours; The Poet's Cat; Edward the Transgressor)*

Ursula Kiernan lives in Storrington, West Sussex. She is a dedicated cat lover. Dogs, too. She has won many poetry competition prizes. Her début collection, *Fish That Sing*, came out in 1999.

Pauline Kirk *(Tippo the Time Lord)*

Born in Birmingham and now living in York, Pauline received a Yorkshire Arts 'New Beginnings Award' in 1995 to become a full-time writer and partner in Fighting Cock Press. Seven collections of her poetry and two novels, *Waters of Time* and *The Keepers*, have been published to date. In 2004 Redbeck Press will be launching her new and selected poems, *Walking to Snailbeach*.

Usha Kishore *(Benjy; Gorrym, The Castle Cat)*

Usha Kishore is a lecturer in English at I.O.M College. She has been published in many poetry magazines and anthologies in the UK, India and Ireland. She has also published critical articles and recently won the Olive Lamming Memorial Poetry Competition, I.O.M. She was regional winner of the Ottaker and Faber Poetry Competition, 2002. She is the mother of twins; one boy, one girl.

Sarah Louise Lill (Bookmark Poem – *The Predator*)

Sarah wrote this poem aged 13 when a pupil at Bingley Grammar School in Bradford. Now a teenager living in Pateley Bridge and attending Nidderdale High School and Community College, her main interests are amateur dramatics, art and swimming.

John Lucas *(A Seasonable Wish)*
John Lucas lives in Nottingham where he is publisher/editor of Shoestring Press. He has had a number of volumes of poetry published himself, including two Redbeck collections: *One for the Piano* and *On the Track*. *A World Perhaps: New and Selected Poems* was published by Sow's Ear Press/Trent Editions at the end of 2002. *The Long and the Short of It*, also via Redbeck Press, will be available from November 2004.

Alexis Lykiard *(Lost; Found; Mr. Cool; Mouse)*
Alexis Lykiard believes human beings, artists particularly, have much to learn from cats. *Cat Kin* (1985 and 1994) – which Ted Hughes considered "contagiously cat-like in all its dextrous twists" – is a favourite among Lykiard's many books. These include most recently, *Jean Rhys Revisited* (Stride, 2000); *Skeleton Keys* (Redbeck, 2003); and in translation *Heliogabalus, or the Anarchist Crowned* by Antonin Artaud (Creation Books, 2003).

Peter Manning (Cover illustration and *Shadow)*
Peter Manning was born in Wales and grew up in Suffolk and Yorkshire. He and his wife Suzanne both retired early from Bradford Council and now live in the Scottish Borders. They have had dozens of cats of varied character over the years, but the most recent one, Shadow, is so remarkable that he inspired both poem and picture.

Fay Chivers Marshall *(Pledge; Cat Five; Rescue Cat)*
Widely published poet with two collections of her own – *and* (Envoi Poets Publications, 1990) and *Mapping the Debris* (National Poetry Foundation, 2000). Work has appeared in magazines such as *Acumen, Envoi, Outposts, South, The Rialto, Poetry Life, Modern Poetry in Translation, Nova Poetica, Diapason* (Russia) and *W.P. Journal of the Arts* (Eire); and various anthologies.

Fay lives in Worthing and has one self-rescue cat, heathcliff, (cat five – last of line). She has been a regional representative for the Poetry Society, is involved in many writing and pro-animal activities, and will never give up on scribbling and cats.

Sally Michel *(Artist illustrations of Vince)*

Sally Michel is a Member of the Society of Wildlife Artists and as such exhibits frequently at the Mall Gallery in London. She drew the illustrations for Pat Earnshaw's book of twenty-three prose poems called *My Cat Vince*, some of which are reproduced by kind permission in this anthology.

Sue Palmer *(Colin, the Cartwheeling Cat)*

Sue Palmer, a former teacher, has written hundreds of textbooks and educational TV programmes about aspects of literacy. She has also run roadshows for children on grammar and spelling, and is well-known in primary teaching circles for her teacher training courses. Although she has had many children's poems published in anthologies and magazines, *Colin, the Cartwheeling Cat* is her first published poem for a grown-up audience. It is intended for performance – with gusto!

Christopher Pilling *(Mohair)*

Christopher Pilling, who was born in Birmingham, now lives in Cumbria. He has published poetry, French translations and plays. Redbeck Press has brought out three books of his poetry; most recently, *In the Pink* (1999) and *Tree Time* (2003).

Jane Ramsden *(Black Jake, a.k.a. the Real Mort)*

Partner to David Tipton, Jane Ramsden is the originator of the idea for *Cat Kist*. She was also the editor, compiler, part-time typist and proof-reader – so felt able to include her single poetic effort in the anthology. Born 1953 in Bradford, she obtained a BA Combined Honours Degree in French and German from London University and is also a qualified reflexologist. Her 'day job' is Human Resources' Advisor with Bradford Council, where she has undertaken various different posts over more than 25 years in personnel, careers advisory and community work. Out-of-hours, the latter still continues through small scale cat rescue work and she is currently running (literally) with 11 cats.

Zoë Redfern-Nichols *(Bookmark Poem – Cat Poem)*

Zoë, now a teenager, wrote *Cat Poem* when she was 9 years old. She lives in Thornton, Bradford – a proud cohabitor with several cats, including one she was a kitten with. Zoë likes music, musicals (including *Cats*), theatre, playing the piano and being with friends. Another literary venture was compiling a book of 101 uses of an umbrella!

Simon Richey *(Cats)*

Simon Richey lives and works in London. His poems have been published in poetry magazines and anthologies as well as in *The Independent.* He has also had a number of them on Radio 3.

K. V. Skene *(CAT can look at a king; CAT and the fiddle; CAT that ate the canary; CAT curiouser and curiouser)*

K. V. Skene is an expat Canadian who lived in England since 1993 – first in Oxford then in the small seaside town of Swanage on the Dorset coast. She is now living temporarily in Cork, Ireland. Her poems have appeared in Canadian, UK., U.S., Australian and Irish publications. In 1999 she was shortlisted in the CBC Canadian Literary Awards Competition. Her pamphlet, *Pack Rat*, was published in 1992 by Reference West (Canada). A book called *fire water* came out in 1994 (Ekstasis Editions, Canada). *The Uncertainty Factor/As a Rock* was published in 1995 by *Tears in the Fence.* *Elemental Mind* (Broken Jaw Press, Canada) was published in 1999 and in the same year Hilton House published a pamphlet, *The Arran Designs and other poems*. Her publication, *Only a Dragon*, won the Shaunt Basmijian Chapbook Award 2002 (Canada) and was published by Micro Prose.

Margaret Speak *(She-Cat; The Tortoiseshell Cat; My Cat)*

Margaret Speak is an adult literature tutor who mainly teaches poetry. Her work has appeared in *Poetry Review, TLS, Mslexia, Writing Women, Dreamcatcher, New Welsh Review* and many others. She published *The Firefly Cage* through Redbeck Press. She has also won prizes in many competitions (including Bridport, Cardiff and Exeter) with both prose and poetry. She is one of the devising team who founded the Yorkshire Open Poetry Competition, and is Co-ordinator of the Yorkshire Poetry Workshop.

Diana Syder *(Cat and Penny Whistle)*

Diana Syder has two solo collections: *Hubble* (Smith-Doorstop) and *Maxwell's Rainbow*, (Smith-Doorstop), a Poetry Book Society recommendation (in which *Cat and Penny Whistle* was previously published). She was awarded a Public Understanding of Science award for her poetry by the Institute of Physics and, in 2002, was a Leverhulme artist in residence in the Electronic and Electrical Engineering Department, University of Sheffield.

Barry Tebb *(The Outer Darkness)*

Barry Tebb was born in Leeds in 1942. His first collection, *The Quarrel with Ourselves*, was praised by John Carey in *The New Statesman* and his work was included in the Penguin anthology, *Children of Albion*. Redbeck Press published his book *The Lights of Leeds* (Selected Poems) in 2000. His *Collected Poems* were published by Sixties Press in October 2003.

David Tipton *(Thai Two; Shut Me In The Attic With The Cats)*

Born in Birmingham, David Tipton has lived in Argentina and Peru but has spent the last 25 years in Bradford. His more recent publications include the novels *Paradise of Exiles* (1999) and *Medal for Malaya* (2002), both from Shoestring Press; a collection of short stories, *Nordic Barbarians* (Redbeck Press, 2003) and the travel-memoir, *A Sword in the Air* (Appliance Books, 2003).

Sara Jane Tipton *(Fat Cat)*

Daughter of David, Jane Tipton was born in Birmingham in 1967 and has lived variously in Lima, Walton-on-the-Naze, Sheffield, London, St. Leonard's-on-Sea and now Bradford again. She has published three books of poetry, the most recent being *Bitterland* (Redbeck, 2000). She has also written plays and fiction.

Michael Tolkien *(Without Tooth and Claw)*

Michael Tolkien, a retired secondary school teacher has lived in Rutland most of his life. Redbeck Press published his verse collections *Learning Not To Touch* (1997), *Outstripping Gravity* (2000) and *Exposures* (2003). A fourth collection is in preparation and will be available from Redbeck in 2005.

José Watanabe *(The Cat)*

Peruvian poet, José Watanabe, born in Trujillo in 1946, published his first book, *Album de Familia* in 1971. His second, *El Huso de la Palabra*, did not appear until 1989 but established him as perhaps the most important South American poet of his generation. *Historia Natural*, his third published book, confirmed his unique talent. *Path Through the Canefields* (from which the poem *The Cat* was taken) was published in 1997 by White Adder Press. It is Watanabe's first collection in English translation by C.A. de Lomellini and David Tipton.

Alan Whitaker *(Tabby and Ginger)*

Alan Whitaker was born near Bradford in 1952 and grew up in Thornton, birthplace of the Brontes. He spent over 20 years as a journalist and is the author of several books, including two collections of poetry. *Snow in June* was published by Redbeck Press in 1999.

Dan Wyke *(Found Poem; Cat Stretching)*

Dan Wyke's poetry has been published in a number of magazines including *Other Poetry, The New Writer, The Rialto* and *Thumbscrew*. He received an Eric Gregory Award in 1999. In his early thirties, he lives in Brighton where he co-ordinates the Reminiscence Service for Age Concern. At the time of writing, he was looking for a publisher for his first collection, *Early Nights*.